ARIES

TAURUS

GEMINI

CANCER

LEO

VIRGO

COSMOPOLITAN®
the complete bedside astrologer

LIBRA

SCORPIO

SAGITTARIUS

CAPRICORN

AQUARIUS

PISCES

Modern Publishing
A Division of Unisystems, Inc.
New York, New York 10022
Printed in Colombia

Photo credits:
Cover photo:
David De Lossy/Image Bank

Interior photos:
THE STOCK MARKET: Steve Prezant pp. 14, 74, 94; C.B.P. p. 58; Richard Steedman p. 72; Michael A. Keller Studios Ltd. p. 92; RB Studio p. 112; George Diebold p. 114; Ariel Skelley pp. 164, 238
TONY STONE WORLDWIDE: James Darrell p. 12; Ken Scott pp. 104, 152; Rick Rusing p. 247
FPG INTERNATIONAL: Bill Losh pp. 32, 132; James McLoughlin pp. 38, 138, 158; Ron Chapple pp. 44, 144; Jim Cummins p. 52: Stephen Simpson p. 62; Dennie Cody p.82; Robert Cundy p. 118; Stephanie Rausser p. 171; Michael Krasowitz p. 174; Michael Goldman pp. 178, 198; Ken Ross p. 191; Telegraph Colour Library p. 212; Rob Gage p. 218
IMAGE BANK: L.D. Gordon p. 18; Marc Romanelli p. 22; Nicolas Russell pp. 37, 98, 137; Johnny A. Ready p. 64; Fernando Diez p. 78; Brigitte Lambert p. 124; G.J. Images pp. 151, 214; Peter Grumann p. 172; Alan Becker p. 192; Rob Van Petten p. 204; Frank Whitney p. 224; Tom King p. 232; Joe Devenney p. 242

SAGITTARIUS written by Nana Cameron; CAPRICORN and PISCES written by Amber May-March; VIRGO, ARIES, AQUARIUS, GEMINI, LIBRA, TAURUS, CANCER, LEO, SCORPIO written by Pat Strickland

Illustrations by Barbara McGregor

Contents

Lucky you! You were born when the sun was in the sign of Aries, the *first* sector of the zodiac wheel. You are a pioneer, boldly blazing a path for others to follow—a trend-setter, never happy to be second best. You take the initiative, like to be dominant in relationships. You accept challenges others fear.

The zodiac is an imaginary belt of sky divided into twelve sectors, each one ruled by a different constellation. Your horoscope is a map of the sky at the moment of your birth. To get a complete picture of you, we'd need to know the placement of the moon, Mercury, Venus and other planets when you arrived in the world. The human body is seventy percent water, and they all exert a subtle "tidal" pull on us. But the sun, as the strongest force in our solar system, is the dominant factor in the horoscope, determining a majority of our traits and interests. That doesn't mean you have no control: you still have the free will to choose how to handle your talents and inclinations. You can accept, reject or adapt them to suit your style and ambitions.

Traditionally, each sun sign is associated with a gender, quality, and element, which describe its basic nature. Aries is a *masculine* sign, made of *cardinal fire.* The masculine designation refers to your active (versus receptive) approach to life. The cardinal quality means you excel at starting things. Fire gives you a blazing spirit of enthusiasm that can kindle echoing sparks in others...or occasionally ignite their fury!

Aries' symbol, the Ram, represents your impulsive and irrepressible nature. You'll climb even the most discouraging path to the heights. You are a breath of spring,

born when the trees are budding back to life. You are forever young!

The red planet Mars, your ruler, is the mythical god of war. It bestows courage, energy, strong desire, and a commanding personality.

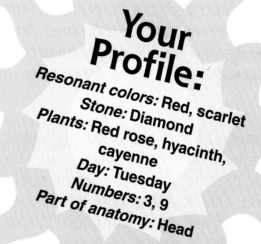

Your Profile:

Resonant colors: Red, scarlet
Stone: Diamond
Plants: Red rose, hyacinth, cayenne
Day: Tuesday
Numbers: 3, 9
Part of anatomy: Head

You are always in demand! Co-workers, friends, and especially the opposite sex flock to you because you're cheerful, witty, and open to trying new places and experiences. You love to make little discoveries. There's a new Thai brewery in town? "Let's give it a jump start," you say. You fill an important need in the lives of friends and loved ones: your far-out ideas for entertainment spice up their lives. And because you are a leader, your crowd falls in with your plans for adventure.

Conversation is one of your greatest pleasures. There's nothing you like better than holding an audience spellbound with details of your latest passion, be it folk art or flamenco. You're delightfully dramatic at these times, which makes it fun for everyone. While you're talking, you can make *anyone* want to try *anything.* (A friend with vertigo may contemplate bungee-jumping if *you* describe it!)

Darling Aries, you're an absolute angel most of the time. But even angels occasionally put their fluffy wings in a closet and let their halos slip a bit. Positive-minded as you are, you can't always feel good or sympathetic. Your mood may slump, when you're forced to deal with too many difficult people or challenging situations. But hang in there; you'll soon find a positive to latch onto again.

Aries is ruled by Mars, the red planet in the midnight sky. Mars represents speed, action and desire. You're always in high gear, but your attention span tends to be short. You become bored easily. That can make it hard for others to share your interests. The second or third time you abandon a pursuit in the middle, friends may conclude you're not the ideal companion for their big plans.

When you first find an exciting new love or job, you're on fire with enthusiasm. But once you've gotten used to the job's routine or the guy's adolescent quirks, you don't have much staying power. Anything new has an excellent chance of capturing your attention.

Generally, you're wise not to waste your time on amusements whose charm has dimmed. But you might enjoy life more, if you'd see projects and commitments through to completion. Few things in life retain their appeal without some sort of lull. And it can be *so* satisfying to admire a job you've done well, or a partnership that's grown stronger through the years.

Admirable Traits
- Fearless
- Generous
- Inspiring
- Confident
- Optimistic
- Pioneering
- Forever youthful

Aggravating Traits
- Reckless
- Overbearing
- Impatient
- Willful

THE OUTER YOU

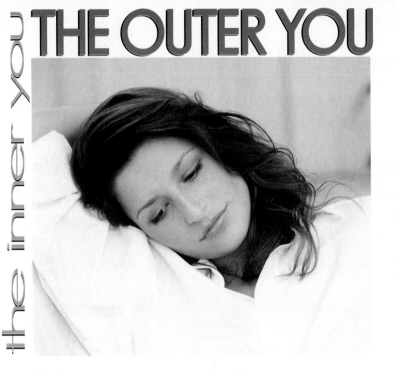

You get a kick out of fashion trends: you always watch them avidly, and often enough, you start them. New colors in cosmetics invariably catch your

to make a splash. But because you're always on the move, you limit you beauty routine to a minimum of time You enjoy up-to-the-minute fashions— especially the quick and easy kind Make-up had better be trendy, eye catching, and long-wearing; who ha time to stop and re-apply?

Red is the magic color for Aries Wear a scarf with a touch of vermil ion, or true-red lipstick (no blu tones). Bright red adds excitemer and drama, and hints at the passion ate woman inside that simple suit.

You are figure-conscious and se dom get seriously out of shape. Stil

> *You enjoy up-to-the-minute fashions—*
> *especially the quick and easy kind.*

eye, as you hurry past the counter in Bloomie's or Saks. You were probably the first in your set to get metallic mascara or a vampy violet lipstick; you love

most of us can benefit from gentl exercise to firm our muscles. Follow simple workout plan, with yoga-typ stretches and deep yogic breathing

It helps you wind down, and your body will quickly respond.

Hair is a big concern for Mars women, because Aries rules the head. You are active and visible at social events, so it's important to look your best. Most of the time you opt for the highest style with the lowest maintenance. But for special occasions, you'll spend the time on a really glamorous style.

Mars girls have a special need for vitamin C. Get yours in tomatoes, oranges, grapefruit and tangerines. If you want to shed unwanted pounds, don't be seduced by fad diets. Just say no to cheese, beer, candy, snack chips, fried foods, and ice cream. Try walking briskly thirty minutes each day. You'll see pleasing results in six weeks.

When a formal occasion is on your social calendar, go all out. You never know who's looking, so why miss an opportunity to shine? You'd look fantastic in a red slip dress or sheath. Add a faceted jet necklace and matching teardrop earrings for dramatic elegance.

The planet ruling your sun sign influences your interests, personality, and inclinations. Here are some ways Mars affects you:

- *Ambitious to succeed*
- *Enthusiastic about life*
- *Impulsive (sometimes to your detriment)*
- *Impatient with delays*
- *Passionate in love*
- *Inspiring to others*
- *Hands-on style*
- *Forceful when necessary*
- *Hardworking*

You're a real go-getter when it comes to money and careers, as well as everything else in life. Recognition is important to the ambitious Mars girl. When you see a chance to make your mark, you're off like a bullet, so you can get there "firstest with the mostest." More often than not, you achieve your goal.

Hard work doesn't faze you. You'll gladly work overtime, if you can expect a big pay-off. Your dazzling creative flair sparkles on the job and in dealing with your co-workers. The best jobs for you offer non-stop activity and frequent changes.

Employers and associates like your direct, cheerful manner, but be careful not to come across as pushy. Mars women are fine in the self-esteem department; it's their sensitivity that occasionally needs a boost. You're wise to focus on your own goals but try to be aware of others' needs and feelings, especially when they're having a rough day. Kindness seldom hurts.

Ruler Mars gives you a strong, independent nature. You'd prefer to be your own boss, and that may eventually be your choice. But self-employment isn't always practical. For now, look for a position where you can control your professional destiny.

With your dynamic personality and many talents, career doors *fly* open. Some fields that beckon to your daring nature are sales, acting, design, politics, firefighting, engineering, journalism, the military, or the entertainment industry.

To fun-loving Aries, money is for pleasure. You're generous with friends and loved ones. You may save for emergencies, but are never stingy. Be sensible, but never cautious. If you are alert to opportunities, you'll reap the rewards. The planets are with you, adorable Aries girl.

Careers to Consider

Certain careers are ideally suited to your sun sign. Here are some you may enjoy:

- *Architect*
- *Surgeon*
- *Athletic coach*
- *Politician*
- *Engineer*
- *Firefighter*
- *Locksmith*
- *Dentist*
- *Law enforcement*
- *Diamond cutter*

With Friends and Family

Your charismatic nature attracts flocks of admirers, so you are seldom lonely. You have the rare ability to communicate with people on any level. As a result, you can have as many friends as you want. Because you're eternally youthful, you enjoy being with youngsters and other active people. You probably also have at least one pet.

don't act like a fragile doll who'll break if not handled with kid gloves. Men you choose to date have a hard time keeping up with your energetic pace.

Men of all ages and backgrounds are drawn by your dynamic style and spirited ways.

Men of all ages and backgrounds are drawn by your dynamic style and spirited ways. They see you as sexy, fun-loving and independent—a powerful combination of traits. This means you can not only have as full a love life as you want, you can also have men as buddies and confidants. They are at ease with you because you

On the job, you're friendly with everyone, and treat people well. But, unless there's someone at work who's really on your mental wavelength, you may not choose to get close to co-workers or superiors.

You enjoy being around other women who are fun, active and interesting. You're surrounded by playmates, but your independent streak may make you unwilling to work at cementing many long-lasting friendships. Look for a few soul mates; you need close friends in your life to add stability.

Family is important to you, but you probably don't choose to spend much time socializing with your parents or siblings. You are there for them when they need you, but you prefer the freedom and adventure of being on your own or doing things with compatible friends.

When it comes to family, you need their love, but not in a clinging or restrictive way. Support is nice, but independence is essential. You expect your relatives to pay attention to what you say and respect your autonomy. And you'll reciprocate; you know the difference between concern and control.

Best Traits

- Childlike enthusiasm
- Eagerness to try new things
- Exciting companionship
- Seldom lean on friends
- Fun ideas

Worst Traits

- Self-absorption
- Pushiness
- "Me first" attitude
- Tendency to neglect old friends
- Insensitivity

ROMANTIC *Profile*

Magnificent Mars girl, you break a lot of hearts as you travel the path to lasting love. If you're a typical Aries girl, you became interested in the opposite sex at an early age. Many of your sun sign sisters marry or have their first serious romantic relationship by age twenty-three.

A passionate zest for life and love makes you eager to sample as many beaux as possible. Your affairs are varied, and the road isn't always smooth. But you survive, and your brave optimism soon guides you to another adventure.

You like to be in charge in romantic situations. Novel approaches to love—and unusual places for it—appeal to you. Passion sizzles in a new setting!

Spontaneity in romance—and other things—is a way of life for you. You feel a need at midnight to see your man right away? You pick up the phone and say, "I'm waiting for you!" The man who stands on ceremony can just stand aside.

> ### Date to die for:
> *Romantic moonlit drive in an open, red convertible*

You travel as much as you can afford, often choosing hot spots that feature exciting night life and other entertainment. You get an urge to go to Vegas or Paris, and quick as a wink, you're on a plane, winging your way to fun. While on vacations or business trips, you meet some fabulous men who adore your fiery spirit. Be sure to invite the best ones to return the visit.

Special Rendezvous:
Behind the grandstand at a July Fourth fireworks display

Your Ascendant Reveals How Others See You

Second in importance to your sun sign, your rising sign determines the image you project. The inner you may be different, but your ascendant guides your automatic reactions to situations.

Aries: bold, impulsive, assertive, independent

Taurus: loyal, stubborn, patient, reliable

Gemini: witty, restless, versatile, talkative

Cancer: moody, cautious, vulnerable, intuitive

Leo: proud, ambitious, passionate, luxury-loving

Virgo: critical, practical, methodical, hardworking

Libra: tactful, refined, intelligent, charming

Scorpio: shrewd, intense, powerful, secretive

Sagittarius: open, restless, cheerful, curious

Capricorn: steady, honest, practical, authoritative

Aquarius: unique, friendly, stubborn, inventive

Pisces: kind, sensitive, adaptable, spiritual

(See Instant Ascendant Locator, p. 252, to locate your rising sign.)

Significant Others

There is no "bad" Sun Sign for the daring Aries girl. But when it comes to building a lasting relationship, some signs suit your needs better than others. Any match can succeed *if both partners really work at it.*

Your Best Bets

Another **Aries** always wants to be number one, which could be a problem, since you do, too. But if the chemistry is right, and each shines in a different area, you can shine together at the top.

Leo will woo you with champagne and gifts. He wants a consort to reciprocate his passion and grace his soirees—a perfect fit. Lovely!

Sagittarius is fun, independent, not terribly reliable. He could be your guy, if you don't depend on him alone for fulfillment.

Gentle **Pisces** can bring romantic fantasies to life. But tread lightly; he may be emotionally fragile. It's worth the effort to keep this relationship on track.

Libra aims to please. His style is full of romantic touches: making love by candlelight to classical music. A high maintenance partner, but worth it.

Aquarius isn't passionate, but he's mentally stimulating. Like you, he craves novelty. Together you may discover a new way of relating.

Worst Prospects

Cancer's moodiness is a nuisance. What have I done *now?* you wonder, as he stomps off looking hurt. Unless you enjoy walking on eggshells, it's likely to be a tough road.

Virgo is orderly; you prefer things *your* way. His raised eyebrow signals that, once again, you've gotten it *wrong.* Better ask yourself: *Do I need this?*

Scorpio is passionate, but has black moods. You both want to dominate. If you work as a team, you can succeed, but when priorities conflict...*duck!*

Your energy makes **Taurus** dizzy. You want to go dancing, then skinny dip till dawn. He spends weekends in his recliner, snacks within reach. Ho hum!

Capricorn is conservative and cares what people think of him. You like your freedom, and to heck with what the neighbors say. If mutual respect exists—and you're willing to let him dominate—it just might work.

Gemini's flighty ways are fun for a while, but for a lifetime? And maybe with offspring? Be wary. His short attention span could become tedious when you're ready to settle down.

The fiery Aries girl is an adventurer at heart, always looking for new interests and new fields to conquer. Vacations and holidays give you opportunities to refresh your mind and meet new people, and you like to make the most of them. You prefer traveling in comfort, but you're seldom ridiculously extravagant.

You are open-minded about lifestyles, and get a kick out of having encounters with most types of men. Whether he's a conservative Capricorn bank manager or an Aquarian beachcomber, he's of interest to you.

Many Arien women are accomplished athletes (take Jennifer Capriati). That's because the daughters of Mars are bursting with natural energy and love coming in first in competitions. If you're not a real pro, chances are you're top-ranked at your club or gym.

Reading is a favorite pastime for Rams. When you can settle down long enough, you love to relax with lively love stories, mysteries, and factual articles. You like to feel you are accomplishing something, so you may read while on your stationary bike or treadmill.

Audio tapes are popular with Aries joggers and commuters. Music of many varieties appeals to you—Philip Glass may be next to Kenny G on your shelf. You know what you like in the realm of art, even if friends and critics don't always agree with your taste.

In your hectic schedule there's little free time, but you find ways to help your favorite charity. Cash gifts, fund raising, and active involvement with children or animals are typical Arien contributions.

Your daily routine is frenetic, so when you have an opportunity for a great escape, you try to shift into a lower gear. A quiet week in a hideaway, alone or with your partner of the moment, is just what you need. Just make sure there's a dance club or casino nearby, in case you get bored with relaxing. After all, you Rams are irrepressible!

Happiest When...

- leading a meeting
- winning any competition
- flirting with a handsome man
- on a daring adventure

Wouldn't Be Caught Dead...

- rocking on the front porch
- driving an old clunker
- being a sore loser
- leaving a party early
- whining about a broken nail

Domestic Style

Most Aries women have jobs or other interests outside the home, but that doesn't diminish your zeal for home life. Your house is your castle, and you're definitely in charge. You expect anyone who shares your home to pitch in with chores *without* being asked. After all, it's in their interest to maintain a pleasant atmosphere.

For you to feel truly comfortable at home, the decor and furnishings must reflect your special interests. When you're surrounded by the things that *mean* something to you, it puts you in a happy mood. The typical Aries residence is a tiny bit showy. Some unusual objects brighten your home — souvenirs of special memories or special people.

Awards and other symbols of any special achievements are proudly displayed. Few Aries women have not collected prizes of one sort or another. Having your trophies in view reminds you of past glories and inspires you to future successes. Your home should include some touches of red—it's your power color.

You enjoy entertaining, especially if someone else does the hard work. You're at your best as the attractively attired hostess; you really shine in the starring role. Fairly simple "dos" are your preference. No need for twenty courses and a different wine with each. You pride yourself on being a ten-minute gourmet chef. Your parties offer good food, plentiful and varied drink, and lots of laughter and lively conversation. Let the good times roll!

Though you love action and enjoy people, there are times when you need to be alone. The perfect retreat for you is any place that lets you breathe clean air and see sights that soothe your busy mind. It may be enough to withdraw briefly to a quiet room, or you may need to travel to a distant mountaintop. Wherever your hideaway, you feel better after a break from any form of stress.

The Aries Cook

Your hectic schedule allows little time for cooking from scratch. You're good with leftovers, though, and creative with cans. You cook spontaneously, often tossing together whatever's in the fridge, and somehow creating a tasty meal. You expect to be praised for your culinary prowess, and you usually are. Invariably, you use a shortcut approach to kitchen duties, and if possible, you leave the cleaning up for someone else!

Ten Years From Now...

Whatever your life's destination, you've probably just arrived. And whether you're the head of a major design house or you've just landed your own newspaper column, you certainly haven't lost sight of your many friends and loyal aides, who helped you get where you want to be. You're a firm believer in gratitude, and now that you're in a position to help friends in return, you do so enthusiastically.

You set your sights way back in kindergarten, and the vision never dimmed. The route may have been tortuous, and probably wound through some wild affairs of the heart. (You meet people from all walks of life; your conquests are liable to include an astronaut or a matador). And you've had your share of setbacks as well (you know what it's like to be scooped after months of dedicated legwork). But nothing was enough to make you veer from your course.

Now you share your glory with your steadfast mate and probably at least one child. You chose your spouse carefully. You knew he'd need loads of self-confidence to be comfortable married to a powerhouse such as you. As CEO of a major corporation, he knows how to handle competition. And he understands your busy schedule. Not that you don't always make time for your loved ones. Friends aren't afraid to turn to you for advice; in fact, you're still the resident expert on their lives!

What's stressful for others is stimulating for you, and your constantly demanding career has taken no toll on your looks. You still look like a million bucks in that tailored scarlet suit—the same size you wore ten years ago! No wonder you amaze admirers and foes alike!

But it's not your style to rest on your laurels. Even if you are running your own business, you're probably plotting what you'll do to top this. There will always be more worlds left to conquer, and you wouldn't have it any other way. You've always liked a challenge—and you know how to set one for yourself!

Potential Pitfalls

Here are a few dangerous tendencies you should work to avoid:

- Marrying in haste
- Wasting cash on faddish items
- Speeding tickets
- Burning too many bridges behind you
- Losing true love through neglect
- Being smug about the future
- Arguments with employers
- Leaving home in a huff
- Not sharing the spotlight with your mate
- Running with the wrong crowd

You can thank your lucky stars! You were born when the sun was in the part of the sky governed by the constellation of Taurus. That gives you loyalty, dependability, and a deep appreciation of beauty. You are a faithful friend and partner, and you always keep your word. Your strength resides in your steady drive and tenacity. Security is an important priority to you.

The zodiac is an imaginary belt that divides the sky into twelve zones. Your horoscope is a map of the sky at the moment you were born. To know *all* your secrets, we'd need a complete natal chart, with the moon, Mercury, Venus, and the other planets in the positions they held at your birth. (The human body is seventy percent water, so all exert a subtle "tidal" pull on us.) But

28

the sun is the strongest force in our solar system and the dominant factor in your horoscope. It determines a majority of your innate tendencies. That doesn't mean you can't control your personality. Free will allows you to handle your talents and inclinations as you wish. You can accept, reject, or adapt any trait to suit your style and ambitions.

By tradition, each sun sign is assigned a gender, quality, and element, which describe its essential nature. Taurus is a *feminine* sign, composed of *fixed earth.* Feminine describes your receptive (as opposed to active) approach to life. The fixed quality confers stability and determination. The earth element means you are practical, grounded in reality.

Like your sign's symbol, the Bull, you are patient and strong-willed. You dig in your heels and refuse to budge, unless the change is your own idea.

Your ruling planet is Venus, mythical goddess of love. It bestows kindness and an appreciation for life's best things. Give you a cozy home, loving mate, tasty meals, a comfy chair, and you're in paradise!

Your Profile:

Resonant color: Blue
Stones: Emerald, jade
Plants: Violet, sage, thyme
Day: Friday
Number: 6
Parts of anatomy: Neck and lower jaw

Be proud, darling daughter of Venus: your love is the enduring and endearing kind. You are a faithful partner and a patient parent, always there when friends or loved ones need comfort or support. Family is important to you, for home is where you feel most secure. You do all you can to make home life pleasant.

Stability and geniality are just two of your many strong points. You are a loyal friend and a dependable employee. You are willing and able to work against great odds. Regardless of frustrations, you stay with a project until it is completed. But this same persistence can turn to stubbornness. Be careful about digging in your heels. If taken to extremes, your tenacity may actually *impede* progress.

You are honest and practical in financial affairs, as in other areas of life. You do your taxes early and thoroughly, itemizing deductions but not digging for loopholes; you're not out to cheat Uncle Sam. In many ways, you're easy to please; your needs are simple, and you are seldom fussy. But sometimes you can be too complacent; there have been times when friends and loved ones wished you were more willing to sample new experiences. You know what you like, but try not to assume that if you haven't tried it, it's not for you.

Although you are a delight to have around most of the time, even a sweet Taurus occasionally loses her cool. When you're angry, you often suppress hurt feelings and brood on your resentment, because you'd rather not initiate confrontations. Beware of this tendency. A woman can only choke down her anger for so long. Sooner or later, you have to let your rage rip, and if it's been building long enough, it can be dangerous. Anyone who's ever seen an angry Taurus fears the danger signal that glints from her eyes. Like the Bull, your nostrils flare; you plant your feet firmly and refuse to budge. It's a rare person who changes your mind, once you've taken a stance on an issue.

Admirable Traits
- Affectionate
- Industrious
- Consistent
- Patient
- Steady
- Reliable
- Thorough

Aggravating Traits
- Possessive
- Habit-bound
- Self-indulgent
- Stubborn

In spite of your tendency to stubbornness, your stability is really a boon to all around you. You have a strong sense of responsibility, and you refuse to let friends down. You create a safety zone in which expectations are always realized. A Taurus may be predictable, but she never disappoints—and that is a great gift.

THE OUTER YOU

look once in a while, to make people look a little closer. Keep your eyes open for new and exciting products in make-up and skin care.

Make simplicity and quality your motto when choosing apparel and hairstyles. Most Venus-ruled gals have curvaceous figures. If your curves are a bit more generous than you'd like, stay with simple lines and fabrics that make you look sleek. Don't go shapeless; it's never an effective disguise.

Born under the influence of Venus, you are naturally interested in being as attractive as possible. You have excellent judgment in selecting clothes, col-

The typical Taurus tends to regard physical exercise as a chore. If that sounds like you, try to find something strenuous you *like* to do—walking

> *Don't be overconfident or get too established in your beauty routine...*

ors, and hairstyles to highlight your best features. But don't be overconfident or get too established in your beauty routine. We can all use a new

swimming, whatever—and do as much of it as you can. Instead of taking the elevator, walk up the stairs. Try simple stretches when you're on the phone. Yoga and dancing are other fun ways to stay limber without feeling like a drudge.

Accent your lovely throat with simple necklaces that draw attention to your face and shapely shoulders. If your neck is a bit short or you have a hint of a second chin (as do many Taureans), wear vee-collars and long chains to give you a pretty line. It's important to moisturize these areas daily to keep them soft and smooth, since they are regularly exposed to the sun's radiation.

Be sure to eat nutritious meals and foods that provide plenty of vitamin C. Oranges, lemons, grapefruit, and tomatoes are some excellent sources. Avoid rich foods and bedtime snacks.

You require a little more sleep than some sun signs. Be sure your pillow is firm enough to support your head and neck without hunching them forward. Your physician or chiropractor can tell you where to find special pillows that do just that. That way you can greet the world with proper Bullish fervor!

Venus, your sun sign ruler, influences your interests, appearance, personality, and romantic inclinations. Here are some ways Venus affects you:

- *Attractive appearance*
- *Appreciation of beauty*
- *Loyalty to friends*
- *Fondness for comfort*
- *Sensuous nature*
- *Relaxing presence*
- *Preference for peaceful places*
- *Enjoyment of art and music*
- *Love of romance*

Money represents material security to you, and security is your main concern in life. You have the ability to save cash at a better rate than most, if you're so inclined. You want to be rich enough to do whatever you like in the future. You feel comfortable only if you have a financial cushion to fall back on in an emergency.

When you buy an expensive item, you want it to last a long time. Durability and quality are important to you. Bulls love bargains, but not on inferior goods. One area where you *refuse* to cut corners is food. You appreciate the best.

In the workplace you are well-liked. Bosses and co-workers respect your diligence and admire your integrity. When necessary, you can work long hours under tremendous pressure. You are driven by your sense of responsibility.

Your idea of a good career is one that provides financial stability. Changing jobs isn't fun for you, as it is for a few sun signs. You thrive in a comfortable job that offers a pleasant work environment, chances for promotion, and a generous vacation schedule.

Freelance work seldom appeals to a Taurus. It's too unpredictable, and requires an enormous amount of enterprise and self-discipline. Neither are you particularly suited to team-work. You are comfortable only with your own pace and priorities. The ability to adapt constantly to a group's work pace and shifting needs eludes Taurus.

You can succeed in many professions, both artistic and sales-oriented. Any occupation that involves the earth, beauty, money, land, or the arts is a likely bet for Taurus.

The forecast for your financial future is excellent, if you make it a habit to put aside cash from each paycheck. Treat it like a bill you owe yourself. Pay yourself first by writing a check to your broker. Pretty soon, you'll have accumulated the security for which you work so hard.

Careers to Consider

Certain careers are ideally suited to your sun sign. Here are some you may enjoy:

- *Art gallery manager*
- *Civil service employee*
- *Cosmetologist*
- *Accountant*
- *Dancer*
- *Singer*
- *Jeweler*
- *Stock broker*
- *Investment consultant*

With Friends and Family

Bulls find more pleasure in constancy than variety. A typical Taurus girl prefers to spend time with proven companions, with whom she feels comfortable, rather than hunt for new friends. You may even be a bit suspicious of strange men who come on to you.

You are an extremely reliable friend. When a close pal asks you to do a favor, you don't let her down. If the casual about time. Being late for appointments is a frequent Taurus problem, especially because you tend not to *see* it as a problem. It is. It's all very well to be laid-back, but not when you're dealing with other people's time. If you respect the person who's

You tend to stick with a few things that have attracted you for a long time.

timing is bad, you may explain that you can't respond right now, but you *will* respond—as soon as possible.

Because your pace of life is a little slower than some, you are rather waiting, you should make an effort to be punctual. It's plain, old-fashioned courtesy.

You get along well with people of all ages and types. Older folks find you particularly pleasant company; you don't hurry them or take over conversations. You are naturally drawn to people whose beliefs, interests, and priorities match your own.

You are not quick to latch on to new issues or activities. You tend to stick with a few things that have attracted you for a long time. Be conscious that others develop new enthusiasms more quickly. If a firm friend finds a new interest that doesn't attract you, try not to feel left out. Show an interest, even if you don't feel it. Ask her about it, or she may end up feeling rejected. The same goes for new acquaintances. Be open to them, and don't regard them as competition. In time you may be drawn to them, too.

Pets play an important part in the life of the average Taurean. When choosing animal companion, select one whose temperament is calm and easy to live with. You can spend many happy hours curled up on the couch with an affectionate pet. But a self-sufficient animal may be a drag, especially if he snubs you when you're in the mood to cuddle.

Best Traits

- Loyalty, sincerity
- Calm, soothing temperament
- Reliability
- Patience, sympathy
- Caring nature

Worst Traits

- Possessiveness
- Stubbornness, dogmatism
- Self-indulgence
- Reluctance to change
- Jealousy

ROMANTIC *Profile*

Sweet as honey and slow as molasses, that's the lovely Taurus lady when she's considering taking a lover. You are a highly sensuous woman, but that doesn't prevent you from being cautious. The man who's offering you a diamond ring had better have a lasting partnership in mind.

Your passions are strong, but so is your earthy common sense. You won't bother to start a relationship that's going nowhere in the morning. You well understand the importance of loyalty and commitment in today's risky romantic climate. You are one of the world's most faithful partners, and you expect your mate to treat you with equal respect.

Making love is relaxation to you. You want romance to be sensuous and easy. Surprises turn you off. You'd rather know what to expect from a partner. You want a slow hand, with a gentle yet firm touch. Fast and furious lovemaking leaves you stressed out. You are turned off by any partner who criticizes your body.

Date to die for:
Romantic candlelight dinner in a cozy country inn

Venus, the planet of love and affection, is your celestial ruler and guiding light. It also represents moral values, and you are committed to yours. You'll be happiest if you don't compromise

your beliefs—in romantic situations or life in general.

The ultimate goal of romance, for you, is to establish a cozy nest for the future. You long to settle down with the right companion and start getting comfortable. Once you do, it's hard to drag you away, even for a pleasure trip. Home is most definitely where you heart is.

Special Rendezvous:
A moonlit mountaintop, with only the stars to light your love

Your Ascendant Reveals How Others See You

Second in importance to your sun sign, your rising sign determines the image you project. The inner you may be different, but your ascendant guides your automatic reactions to situations.

Aries: bold, impulsive, assertive, independent

Taurus: loyal, stubborn, patient, reliable

Gemini: witty, restless, versatile, talkative

Cancer: moody, cautious, vulnerable, intuitive

Leo: proud, ambitious, passionate, luxury-loving

Virgo: critical, practical, methodical, hardworking

Libra: tactful, refined, intelligent, charming

Scorpio: shrewd, intense, powerful, secretive

Sagittarius: open, restless, cheerful, curious

Capricorn: steady, honest, practical, authoritative

Aquarius: unique, friendly, stubborn, inventive

Pisces: kind, sensitive, adaptable, spiritual

(See Instant Ascendant Locator, p. 252, to locate your rising sign.)

Significant Others

There is no "bad" sun sign for tender Taurus girls. But when it comes to building a lasting relationship, some signs suit your needs better than others. Any match can succeed *if both partners are willing to work at it.*

Your Best Bets

Romance with another **Taurus** means life is predictable, but that's okay. You both value comfort and beautiful possessions, are sensuous and conservative. It's safe. Others might find it dull, but you crave familiarity the way other signs crave excitement.

If you can accept **Cancer's** moodiness and conquer the communication gap, this match can work. Both want security and are willing to work to create a harmonious home life.

Partnership with a **Virgo** brings stability and a robust love life. He's rather fussy, but you can deal with it; at least he's consistent. Your practicality and reliable love soothe his nerves.

Libra gives you so much attention, you'll think you're in heaven. The sensual side is irresistible. But watch out for your possessive streak. He'll flirt, but he's not going anywhere—unless he senses you tightening the reins.

Capricorn is strong, dignified, and earthy in romance. You love it! This could be a great relationship.

You and **Pisces** are sensuous and know how to satisfy each other. He also shares your desire for a comfortable home life. Together, you should find true contentment.

Worst Prospects

Gemini's restless ways and mental approach to everything make you uncomfortable. You're set in your ways, and he's always trying on new ideas and interests—sometimes in other women!

Scorpio's possessive and passionate nature doesn't suit you. He's looking for emotional intensity; you're too sensible for him. And you'll never be at ease with him when his mood hits bottom.

Aquarius is too unpredictable for you. He wants total freedom; you want someone there by your side. If anything clicks between you, it's purely accidental.

Sagittarius is a bachelor at heart. He likes the comforts you give, but doesn't reciprocate. His idea of fun is physical activity; yours is a cuddle on a comfy couch. You won't find much you can do together.

Leo and you have will powers strong enough to move mountains. But most of the time you're pushing in opposite directions. You'll get nowhere that way.

Aries gets bored when life is too predictable. You want stability; he craves excitement and novelty. It would be tough to make this work.

Emotional security, money, and material possessions are your passions. Your need for reliability rules your daily life. So you'll cheerfully spend some of your free time work-ing overtime if it will enhance your sense of security.

That doesn't mean you horde money. Generosity comes naturally to you. You give money, time, or clothing you no longer wear to your favorite charity. Many Taurus women prepare bags filled with canned goods and other grocery items to give to needy families. Others do volunteer work in hospi-tals and shelters for homeless fami-lies. Whatever your favorite cause, you have a soft spot in your heart for those less fortunate than you.

When you do give yourself a break, your pleasures are simple.

Music is a source of delight for most Taurus girls; whatever else you do for fun, you usually have something playing in the background. You enjoy eating (and maybe cooking) delicious meals. Food is one of the few areas where novelty appeals; you may go out of your way to try a new restaurant. Of course, you're also very loyal to proven places where you've had great gastronomi-cal experiences before.

Travel appeals to you only if you know where you'll be staying and can plan ahead. You'll take an occasional trip for business or pleasure, but in general you don't feel the need to go out of your way to find enjoyment. You actually prefer to relax in the comfort of your own cozy nest. When you do travel, you want everything to go exactly as planned, with no surprises along the way. (Lost luggage and waiting out long delays in airports are your idea of torture.) So you never leave the arrangements to chance.

The typical Taurus gal's favorite sport is a lively bedroom workout. If forced to exercise, you'll opt for a walk, a little golf, or volleyball.

Travel tip: Tahiti or the Fiji Islands is a wonderful escape for a sensuous woman like you. The islanders' laid-back approach to life can inspire you to find new and simpler ways to spend your free time. Who knows? You may even fall in love and forget to come back to the office after your vacation ends.

Happiest When...
- having breakfast in bed
- choosing a new recliner
- showing off your garden
- admiring your favorite painting
- snoozing after a night of love

Wouldn't Be Caught Dead...
- jogging at dawn
- swearing off chocolate
- offering to babysit for a week
- cha-cha-ing at Chico's Hideaway
- on a bicycle tour of anywhere

Domestic Style

Venus's daughters are the most sensuous women on the planet. You take delight in physical pleasures, whether for the touch, eyes, ears, nose, or tastebuds. Your cuddly body is built for pleasure!

You adore dining with friends or loved ones in a scenic setting. The more senses you can employ at once, the better you like it. You're in seventh heaven when a lover serves you breakfast (or any other meal) in bed. Backrubs are practically a religious experience for you.

You thrive in a pleasant atmosphere, particularly at home. You need stability and creature comforts in order to feel confident at home. If you don't get them in your home life, you'll be unsettled in other areas as well. You want things to be where you've put them, and loved ones to be there when you need them.

Home furnishings reflect your special interests and reveal a great

deal about you. You appreciate attractive artwork and fine accessories. Everything in your home is arranged for comfort: large lamps, oversized chairs, and (with luck) a fireplace form ideal settings for curling up and relaxing.

Taurus is associated with the earth, and you need to be close to it. You can relax in a garden, a country inn, a quiet park, or any other environment where you're in close touch with Mother Nature. Your ideal retreat provides your favorite comfort foods, a huge bed, and lots of time for sleeping (or, if you're in the mood, lovemaking). Blue is your power color. Be sure to have at least a small touch of this calming hue in each room of your home.

Your idea of a perfect party includes enough food to feed a battalion of hungry men, a refrigerator bursting with beverages, and plenty of comfortable seats. Your favorite

guests are those you don't have to worry about impressing.

The Taurus Cook

Anyone lucky enough to be invited to dine at your home seldom refuses. Great gourmet chefs such as James Beard were born under your sign. Your kitchen is a comforting place, featuring wonderful spices and a full refrigerator. You concoct delicious meals that make guests' mouths water. Even when no company is coming, you take trouble over meals. You choose ingredients carefully. Meat and potatoes are popular with Bulls. Desserts are one of your specialties.

Ten Years From Now...

If you haven't yet made your first million, you are at least on the road to substantial wealth. Your most recent property acquisition—a luxury hotel or condominium building—promises to be not only a steady source of income, but a useful possession (it's an ideal place for romantic tête-à-têtes for your jet-set buddies). Your expertise in matters of comfort is apparent in every aspect of whatever business you're in.

After finding your dream home and furnishing it to suit your style, you can concentrate on creating a happy family to fill it. If you're not already settled into marriage, your strong sense of family will be prodding you to pick a partner. Look for a man with his feet on the ground and his head firmly on his shoulders. If he appreciates your extraordinary knack for providing comfort, you'll have found your match. Now you're ready for a spell of homemaking. Baking brownies for a cuddly three-year-old and her hunky Dad is a favorite pastime. But you still don't let it interfere with your dedication to business. Your job is still your security, whether it's real estate or swapping on the stock exchange, and it's still a top priority. Something has to pay for all that Valrhona ® chocolate!

You have an excellent reputation in your chosen field, and you've frequently rejected job offers, preferring to stay where you're already established. Don't forget to make use of those offers, though—they can be very useful as leverage to get you that well deserved raise or promotion.

Chances are there's a big corporation courting your professional favors. But it may require a temporary move. Can you bear to take six months away from home to pick up that fat consulting fee? You'd turn it down if you felt you could afford it; true to form, you'd still rather be at home. But it would be a nice little boost for your ever-growing nest egg. Besides, you wouldn't mind another chance to sample the culinary delights of the Continent....Ah, it's a sweet life for you. Enjoy it!

P o t e n t i a l   P i t f a l l s

Here are a few dangerous tendencies you should work to avoid:

- Becoming set in your ways
- Valuing things more than people
- Jobs that fail to challenge you
- Tunnel vision
- Being smug about your partner
- Neglecting to see some of the world
- Hiding feelings to avoid being hurt
- Bearing grudges
- Being a slave to your appetites
- Insensitivity to others' feelings

Clever Gemini, you were born when the sun was in the sign of the Twins, linked to wit and mental acuity. You are a born communicator with an opinion on any subject. A restless lady, you need your career—and everything else—to give you intellectual breathing space. Changeable you may be, but never boring!

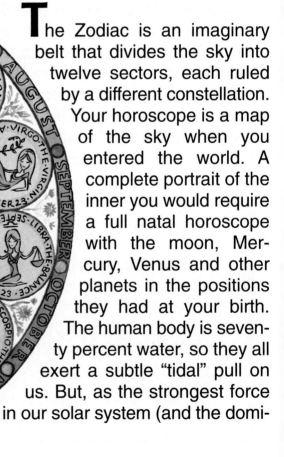

The Zodiac is an imaginary belt that divides the sky into twelve sectors, each ruled by a different constellation. Your horoscope is a map of the sky when you entered the world. A complete portrait of the inner you would require a full natal horoscope with the moon, Mercury, Venus and other planets in the positions they had at your birth. The human body is seventy percent water, so they all exert a subtle "tidal" pull on us. But, as the strongest force in our solar system (and the dominant factor in your horoscope), the sun determines a majority of your traits and interests. That doesn't mean you can't resist its pull: you choose how and how much to use your talents and inclinations. You can reject, accept or adapt them to suit your will and desires.

Based on its position in the zodiac wheel, each sun sign has a gender, quality and element, which describe its essential nature. Gemini is a masculine sign, made of mutable air. Masculine refers to your active (as opposed to receptive) character, while mutable means you are adaptable, and air gives you a mental orientation. Your most important activity occurs within your mind.

The Twins are Gemini's symbol, representing the duality of your versatile nature. You can be angelic on Sunday and devilish on Monday. You are bright and fun-loving, but you also have a serious side.

Mercury is your ruling planet. Named for the mythical messenger of the gods, it is the mental planet. You have a good mind, a strong curiosity, and quicksilver reactions to people and situations.

Your Profile:

Resonant color: Luminous yellow
Stone: Pearl
Plants: Jasmine, heather, lavender
Day: Wednesday
Number: 4
Parts of anatomy: Shoulders, arms, hands, lungs

Always adaptable, you are a born communicator, with an opinion on every subject. Mercury, the mental planet and your celestial ruler, imparts a keen mind and a bright sense of humor: you can find something amusing in almost any situation. Some people mistake this trait for lack of feeling, but you're not callous. It's just that you have a sharper wit than most.

Your life purpose is to learn all you can and to make mental connections. Like Agatha Christie's Miss Marple, you have an uncanny knack for insightful associations. You can leap to conclusions based on a momentary impression—and you're almost always right! It's great fun and can be extremely useful.

Gemini is represented by the Twins—a dual sign, which means you have two very different sides to your personality. You're a bit of a Dr. Jekyll and Ms. Hyde, which can be confusing to your friends and loved ones. In the morning, you're snappish; in the evening, chatty and cheerful—or vice versa. While this makes living with you a bit tricky, it also makes you fascinating. And it means that you're never in a bad mood for long.

Your versatile mind allows you to be more objective than most signs. You have many and varied interests. You may be passionate about baseball and opera, Shakespeare and Anne Rice. You adore gossip (admit it!), but not in a malicious way. It's merely that you're terribly curious...and other people's lives can be so entertaining!

Gemini gals are good story-tellers and, when necessary, convincing fibbers. All of this makes you a fabulous conversationalist. You're on everyone's guest list. And you'll stay there, in spite of being rather cavalier about invitations, because when you do show up, nobody's ever bored.

You are one of the zodiac's great thinkers. You approach everything from a mental angle. You're a natural at networking and can quickly catch on to fresh ideas and unusual people. Relating is easy for you; you are inherently sociable. You greet everything with an open mind, and others sense your tolerance. You like people, so they like you.

Admirable Traits
- Versatile
- Logical
- Communicative
- Jill-of-all-trades
- Sociable
- Perceptive
- Tolerant
- Resourceful

Aggravating Traits
- Restless
- Impatient
- Changeable
- Devious
- Dualistic

Restless Gemini girls lead a full, active life. You often run on nervous energy when you need sleep. To curb this tendency, establish a relaxing bedtime routine to calm and shift your mind into low gear. Follow it nightly. Your brain will recognize it and begin to relax. Yoga, meditation, poetry and prayer are excellent relaxation techniques. Don't read a mystery or do aerobics at night; they're too stimulating.

Your hands and arms may suffer from excessive exposure to damaging winds and sunlight. Protect them, and when they do get dry, use moisturizer often and avoid harsh soap. You need exercise to keep your tri-

You're a lucky lady, for your power planet, Mercury, gives you long-lasting inner youth. A childlike receptivity keeps you active, responsive and

A childlike receptivity keeps you active, responsive and enthusiastic all your life.

enthusiastic all your life. You love to discover new pastimes; when you do, you want to proclaim them to the world.

ceps firm and toned. Fortunately, you enjoy sports, so this is no hardship. Recommended for the purpose are golf, fencing, tennis and volleyball.

Gemini rules the lungs. You are very susceptible to lung damage from tobacco smoke—first or secondhand. If you're a smoker or live with one, do your best to eliminate the habit from your home. It not only harms the inner body, it also dries out your face, makes you look older, and causes those "pucker" wrinkles around your lips.

To control weight, get in the grazing habit. Eat six low-calorie "meals" throughout the day, instead of big meals. Limit each to no more than 250 calories. Fresh fruit and vegetables are ideal.

When choosing clothes and cosmetics, your best bets are colors that flatter your skin tone. If you do wear kinky colors, don't try to match your makeup to your outfit. Instead, use shades that complement your complexion. You have pretty skin; call attention to it.

Mercury, your planetary ruler, influences your looks, interests, personality, and love nature. Here are some ways Mercury affects you:

- *Youthful looks at any age*
- *Mental alertness*
- *Enthusiasm for learning*
- *An "idea" person*
- *Attracted to smart men*
- *Good with your hands*
- *Loathe boring jobs*
- *Impatience with slower minds*
- *Tendency to do two things at once*
- *Persuasive speaking ability*

Your renowned adaptability can be a double-edged sword. On the plus side, you are more employable than highly specialized signs—and more likely to be happy where you end up. On the minus side, you may take the easy road and never develop your special talents, which could be outstanding. Success beckons in creative careers such as acting, writing, teaching, public relations, or the entertainment industry.

You do best in a field that encourages self-sufficiency, holds your attention, and offers intellectual space. Many Geminis like to move around from job to job, or even city to city. Whatever your style, be smart and concentrate on one or two fields; it's hard to advance if you're constantly making lateral moves. Focus your efforts on the career that appeals most.

Managers and co-workers like the way you quickly catch on to new ideas and work methods. You do many things well. But watch your step when chatting in the workplace. Gossip or sarcasm could cause your downfall. Few people have as broad a sense of

humor as you, and you never know who's linked to whom in the business world. Sassy talk has a way of being repeated, often to the wrong person.

Thrift is not part of your make-up. You like to enjoy your income, and have many hobbies and interests. If you gamble, you'd be smart to limit your bets, so the excitement of the game doesn't seduce you out of more cash than you can afford.

If you keep your eye on the future, you will move higher on the ladder of success, with raises and promotions on every rung. Still, you'd be wise to get in the habit of saving some of your earnings for future needs. In the next few years, Saturn tests your values and financial savvy. Everything should go smoothly, if you get your saving and spending habits under control A.S.A.P.

Careers to Consider

Certain careers are ideally suited to your sun sign. Here are some you may enjoy:
- *Writer*
- *Allergist*
- *Book seller*
- *Mechanical engineer*
- *Journalist*
- *Computer programmer*
- *Graphologist (handwriting expert)*
- *Secretary*
- *Airline industry employee*
- *Nerve specialist*

With Friends and Family

The Gemini girl is one of the friendliest in any group. Your circle of acquaintance expands at will. A restless nature makes you set a fast pace in your social life. You're impatient with slow speakers, and may even finish sentences for them. To feel at ease with a friend or potential lover, you must find him amusing, intelligent and mentally stimulating. You may have a preference for younger pals because they can match your all-out enthusiasm.

meet. Friendship, to you, is sharing good times—not heart-to-hearts and constant emotional support. You prefer to be free and unencumbered, so you can take advantage of your infinite options.

You like to go and come as you

Friendship, to you, is sharing good times—not heart-to-hearts and constant emotional support.

All your many friends would like to be close to you, but your social style keeps most at a little distance. You'll never be really cozy with many, because you can't sit still long enough to open up to everyone you

please, in romance as well as friendship. Not everyone willingly allows this freedom; critics may conclude you don't truly care about them. Of course, that's not true. You do care—just not at the expense of everything else. You're not the emotional type.

56

You're too intelligent and alert to get carried away. Logic rules your life.

You're very persuasive, and on those rare occasions when a problem arises, you can usually talk your way out of the blame. Because you easily become bored, you simply avoid people you consider dull. You may not realize it (it's just your nature), but you tend to keep even intimate relationships on a rather superficial level. You seldom, if ever, choose to fence yourself in.

You can enjoy being with anyone who is mentally stimulating. Age and gender aren't important criteria for good companionship. You are fascinated by certain pastimes and subjects, and get a kick out of exchanging views and information with people who share those interests.

Best Traits

- Open-minded and tolerant
- Great communicator
- Full of ideas
- Eclectic activities
- Perceptive

Worst Traits

- Talk, talk, talk!
- Nervous and restless
- Detached and unemotional
- Impatient with slow thinkers
- Superficial in relationships

ROMANTIC *Profile*

You're so busy expanding your horizons, it seldom occurs to you that it might be nice to have a steady beau. Steady isn't really your style. There's always some man around who'd adore sharing a spicy evening with you. Who wants to limit her options? Not you!

Mercury, the mental planet, is your ruler, so anyone who hopes to win your heart must first stimulate your mind. It's not that you lack interest in physical pleasures. Far from it! But your agile mind and restless nature require more than that. You want to know there'll be an exciting exchange of ideas before and after any physical fireworks.

Routine in romance is anathema to you. You want amorous experiences to be varied, lighthearted, and stimulating. You're turned off by partners who cling. You lose all respect for a mate who begs for pity when you want to end the relationship.

Gemini girls are always on the go, you just love to travel. You have the strongest sense of curiosity in the zodiac family. You delight in learning new things, and you must experience them firsthand, from the pyramids of Egypt to a new yoga technique.

Date to die for:
A light champagne supper after a sexy foreign film

With all your contacts and busy schedule, you have myriad opportunities to socialize. If you aren't romantically "attached", friends and co-workers probably get a kick out of teasing you about settling down. It doesn't bother you. They don't seem to realize that settling down is not one of the Gemini Butterfly's serious goals. You're having far too much fun playing games—and probably flirting with their guys!

Special Rendezvous: in the locked library of a Victorian mansion

Your Ascendant Reveals How Others See You

Second in importance to your sun sign, your rising sign determines the image you project. The inner you may be different, but your ascendant guides your automatic reactions to situations.

Aries: bold, impulsive, assertive, independent

Taurus: loyal, stubborn, patient, reliable

Gemini: witty, restless, versatile, talkative

Cancer: moody, cautious, vulnerable, intuitive

Leo: proud, ambitious, passionate, luxury-loving

Virgo: critical, practical, methodical, hardworking

Libra: tactful, refined, intelligent, charming

Scorpio: shrewd, intense, powerful, secretive

Sagittarius: open, restless, cheerful, curious

Capricorn: steady, honest, practical, authoritative

Aquarius: unique, friendly, stubborn, inventive

Pisces: kind, sensitive, adaptable, spiritual

(See Instant Ascendant Locator, p. 252, to locate your rising sign.)

Significant Others

There is no "bad" sun sign for gregarious Gemini girls. But when it comes to building a lasting relationship, some signs suit your needs better than others. Any match can work *if both partners are willing to work at it.*

Your Best Bets

Partnership with another **Gemini** can be fun, with all the activities and mental energy you both have. His light-hearted style suits you—in the bedroom and out. The many books and magazines in your home reflect your common interests.

Libra is beguiled by your wit and intelligence. You find him charming and gracious. The match may lack something, but life is sure to be fun. (P.S. He's as big a flirt as you.)

Life with **Taurus** brings stability and earthy sex. He tends to be a bit conservative, but you know how to loosen him up.

Pisces is deep, mysterious, and emotional. You're a logical thinker. If you can find your way through the fog, this could be an interesting match.

Sagittarius is independent and direct. You team up for lots of merry adventures...but who's watching the children, if it gets that far?

Aquarius has never met a woman so easy to get along with. You've never met a man so crazy. A good match.

Worst Prospects

Scorpio's passionate, possessive nature doesn't suit you. He's looking for emotional intensity; you don't have it. As soon as his mood hits bottom, you're out the door.

Aries has a temper that shakes the rafters. You want to talk things out. Life together is a series of challenges. The match has possibilities, but is very complex.

Leo is liable to bore you; he's too predictable. He needs applause and daily reassurance that he's king. The sex may be great, but he takes lots of emotional maintenance.

Any **Cancer** man who marries a Gemini girl must be a masochist. You're all intellect; he's all emotion. Unhappy for both.

Capricorn expects loyalty and dependability—not your strong suits. His public image is precious to him; he needs a partner who'll play by the company's rules. You'll never understand each other.

Virgo wants everything exactly as he thinks it should be. You get bored if expected to stick with a task too long. He's asking for trouble if he asks for your hand.

Passionate Interests

You have so many interests that you sometimes have trouble focusing on one at a time. You're liable to begin so many projects that some of them never get finished. Reading, writing, collecting (books and other reading material, miniatures, autographs) are favorite hobbies of Mercury's children. Walking and jogging are popular physical pursuits.

Whatever you do for fun, you become immersed in it. Since Mercury rules communication, many Geminis enjoy citizen's band radio, shortwave radio, or even listening to police scanners. Television is a must—especially programs that offer food for thought. The instantaneous connection with distant people appeals to Mercury's child. Travel, pen pals, flying, skydiving,

and photography are also popular. Twins are creative in many ways: you may enjoy acting or doll making. Jazz and rock music are at the top of your musical charts.

Travel appeals to Mercury girls; it's the best way to satisfy your huge curiosity about the world. You prefer to take an airplane when going a long distance. You want to be at your destination A.S.A.P., so you can be off to the next one!

You dream of going off on a great escape; exotic sights and people beckon. The super-civilized bustle of London is equally appealing. (You could have a grand time in pubs, chatting up British hunks between dart games; the lighthearted mood is ideal for flirting.) The truth is, you want to see it all!

You have a soft spot in your heart for several favored causes. You are drawn to the campaign to promote literacy, because you know the fun and opportunities available only through the written word.

Reading for the blind is another pet project. Because you get so much pleasure from reading, you get great satisfaction from bringing books to life for those who have lost their sight.

Happiest When...
ᛘᚸ rereading your favorite book
ᛘᚸ being courted by two men
ᛘᚸ showing off your knowledge
ᛘᚸ discovering a new interest
ᛘᚸ flirting at a party

Wouldn't Be Caught Dead...
ᛘᚸ at a book burning
ᛘᚸ taking a vow of silence
ᛘᚸ giving up reading
ᛘᚸ playing checkers every Tuesday
ᛘᚸ at a weight-loss camp

Domestic Style

You need a home that's large enough for you to roam around in when you're feeling restless. The typical Gemini woman craves the sophisticated variety of activities available in a large city. Home, to you, is the place you relax after a full day. Although you might not spend as much time there as some, you want it to provide easy living and be inviting to your friends.

Comfort means bright, cheerful decor and furnishings that put you in a good mood. Books, magazines, movie videos, compact discs or audio tapes pack the Mercury girl's abode, the legacy of the communication planet. Your brain wants constant stimulation. Whenever you get the chance, you like to relax with your favorite form of recorded entertainment.

For a party to be a success in your eyes, its guests must be witty, intelligent and stimulating. Decorations, drinks, and menu are not as important as food for thought. Society is a marketplace of ideas, in your view. You spend much more time contemplating the guest list than the menu.

(You have so many aquaintances to choose from!)

With your active mind, boredom is rare. There's always something to think about. You fill up 'down time' with pondering some puzzling question or thinking up your next project. Planning is half the fun. You enjoy being alone for a while each day to read, make plans or just think.

If you live with anyone, you need a private retreat. To think clearly, twins require privacy, a place that offers escape from the clamor of family life. The perfect haven for a Gemini thinker is a home library, with a door that locks from the inside. Some harried moms withdraw to a locked bathroom to enjoy a quiet bubble bath. (Take your boom box along to mask outside noise.) Once you find your quiet place, you'll use it often.

The Gemini Cook

Food is not a focal point for you. With your busy schedule, you're lucky to find enough time to make a "scratch" meal. Guests invited to dinner at your home know there'll be lots of bright conversation and laughs, but probably little home cooking. You know if you waited until you had time to cook, you'd never have anyone over at all. Gemini hostesses like to serve finger foods—they're fun and tasty, and provide variety. When you're alone, you'd rather grab a yogurt or apple, rather than sit down to a six-course meal.

Ten Years From Now...

Airport baggage handlers in Rome, Paris, London, Berlin, Madrid, Kiev, and Singapore have left their mark on your Louis Vuitton luggage. But you wouldn't part with a single scuff; they're all souvenirs of the fabulous times you've had along the way! You've exchanged ideas with people of every race, class, and political belief. You may have been the very first person to get a genuine guffaw from a guard at Buck House. (He was probably a Gemini, too!)

Your travels have included numerous—and varied—roads to romance: a computer whiz, a Swiss banker, or a Pulitzer prize-winning war correspondent is liable to be on the list. (Romantic sessions atop China's Great Wall, or in a TV newsroom, are among your favorite memories.) Of course, when they got serious, you hightailed it for the border...any border! You have to be free to do your own thing.

Success is practically guaranteed to Mercury's clever, logical, and *energetic* child. If you haven't written or directed a Broadway success, you've probably made a fortune selling swimming pools in Arizona, or bagels in Texas. (With your brains and enthusiasm, you can sell *anything* to *anyone!*) You have a knack for finding pleasure in your work, and that's a sure recipe for success in any field.

Never one to rest on your laurels, you are on the verge of making a big decision. Should you accept that teaching post at Oxford's Trinity College? Or would you be happier as a news anchor at CNN? Maybe it's time to write the series of gothic novels you've thought about for so long. Then again, you could have a baby or open a Rodeo Drive boutique.

Decisions, decisions! Choose one, choose two...try not to go for too many more, or you may never complete any of them. Even the zodiac's wonder woman has her limits!

P o t e n t i a l   P i t f a l l s

Here are a few dangerous tendencies you should work to avoid:

- Marrying a man without a sense of humor
- Putting the wrong things in writing
- Settling for laughs when you really want love
- Lacking direction in your career
- Scattering your energy too broadly
- Losing good friends due to neglect
- Ignoring your spiritual needs
- Losing touch with your roots
- Talking when you should listen
- Taking good health for granted

Complex and caring, you were born when the sun was in the part of the sky ruled by the constellation of the Crab. That makes you a sun sign Cancer—one of the most complicated characters of the zodiac. There's a lot

going on under your radiant surface, and it's hard to penetrate, for a strong defense system shields your sensitive feelings.

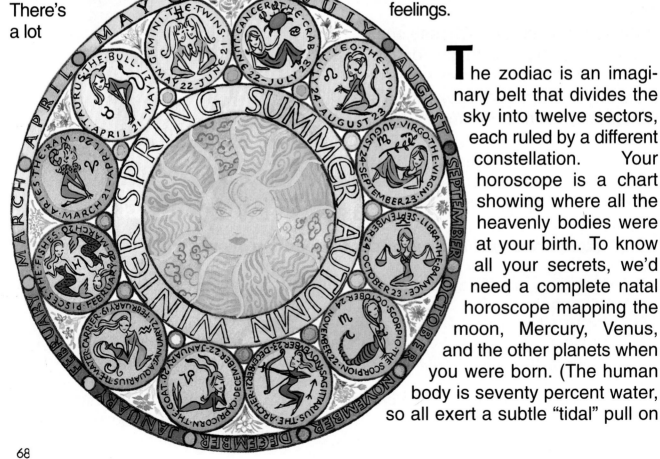

The zodiac is an imaginary belt that divides the sky into twelve sectors, each ruled by a different constellation. Your horoscope is a chart showing where all the heavenly bodies were at your birth. To know all your secrets, we'd need a complete natal horoscope mapping the moon, Mercury, Venus, and the other planets when you were born. (The human body is seventy percent water, so all exert a subtle "tidal" pull on us.) As the sun is the most powerful force in the solar system and the dominant factor in a horoscope, it determines the majority of our traits. Of course, you have the free will to choose how to handle your talents and tendencies – accepting, rejecting or adapting them to suit your style and ambitions.

Traditionally, each sun sign has been assigned a gender, quality and element, which describe its essential nature. Cancer is a *feminine* sign, made of *cardinal water.* The feminine designation means you have a receptive (as opposed to active) temperament; cardinal makes you a "doer"; the water element means you are emotionally oriented. You have the ability to soften people up, or to wear them down, the way water erodes rocks.

Cancer's symbol, the Crab, has a protective shell covering soft flesh underneath. It represents your self-protective nature and your tenacity.

Your ruler is the silvery moon— the only non-planetary ruler in the zodiac. It is associated with the home, emotions, and intuition. You are guided by instincts, and you need a safe base of operations. The moon's swiftly changing phases resemble your changing moods.

Your Profile:

Resonant colors: Sea green, silver, violet
Stones: Moonstone, pearl
Plants: Larkspur, water lily
Day: Monday
Numbers: 2, 3, 7
Parts of anatomy: Breasts, stomach

Shy? Moody? Touchy? All of these words are sometimes used to describe Cancer's nature. And how it must offend you, sweet daughter of the moon, to hear yourself so misunderstood. True, you are sensitive, but there are many other wonderful facets to your complex character. You care about your family and friends far more than they will ever know – for you'll never tell them! Your fragile outer shell is easy for all to see, but few understand the strength hidden inside it.

Your sensitivity is your secret strength. You may be super-susceptible to slights, but your unusually vivid responses work in positive ways as well. Your sensitivity enables you to understand the needs of others; it gives you the capacity to care. Only Scorpio and Pisces have any real understanding of what makes you tick.

Once you have made a friend or decided to love someone, you stick with that person through the toughest times. You may not enjoy it, but you'll be there. In spite of *your* amazing staying power, some people find it hard to maintain a long-term relationship with a Moon Girl. That's because you tend (perhaps unconsciously) to manipulate people through guilt. "After all the things I've done for you..." is a classic Cancer refrain. A very effective ploy, since no one can deny your generosity. But try to remember that your kindnesses were freely given. Too much guilt can create resentment in a formerly grateful friend.

The number one need in your life is a home or base of operation all your own, somewhere you feel in charge and emotionally secure. This doesn't mean you like housework, or that you never go out. It means you need a safe haven. You feel pain more strongly than most, and must have the time and place to lick your wounds. Not that you can't defend yourself. You may not be as aggressive as your Aries sister, but when serious trouble arises, you can hold your position against all odds.

Just beware: Cancerians tend to look for slights. Try not to weigh offenses too heavily, or loved ones may feel they have to watch every word they say, for fear of offending. Remember, some things are said and done offhand, without any hurtful intent. If you attach deep personal meaning to unintentional wrongs, you may cut off a worthwhile relationship. Try to look at the bright side, darling moon girl. We do appreciate your caring ways.

Admirable Traits
- Intuitive
- Responsive
- Imaginative
- Creative
- Romantic
- Expressive
- Patriotic

Aggravating Traits
- Moody
- Possessive
- Self-protective
- Supersensitive
- Lives in the past

the inner you

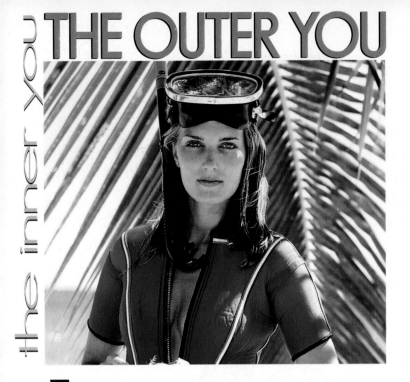

Everything that's beautiful fascinates you; that's one reason you always try

nent in your wardrobe. Plushy textures and fuzzy knits emphasize you cuddly nature.

Soft, romantic hairstyles suit you type of feminine beauty. Your natura ly good complexion retains its fin texture throughout your entire life Although you enjoy displaying you beauty, you're seldom flashy —an never garish—in your choice o clothes or cosmetics.

You are always diet-conscious, bu being a water sign, you tend to hol fluid more easily than other signs. T

> *Your home should contain a special hideaway, where you can catch your breath and relax in peace.*

to look your best. You are very aware of others' looks, so you figure they must be aware of yours. Soft, heathery colors become you: dusty rose and Wedgwood blue should be promi-

stay as svelte as you like, avoid ric foods and refined sugars. Be sure eat lots of fresh fruit and vegetable to provide your active body with th necessary minerals and nutrients.

Moon girls tend to be softly curvy in appearance. To prevent your curves from turning into bulges, regular exercise is highly recommended. Isometrics and gentle stretches are suitable for your needs. Swimming is a favorite sport for many Crab ladies. Walking and bicycling are also popular.

Your sensitive nature does best when you have had sufficient sleep. Going without rest can make you cranky and irritable. When you're under stress for an extended period, you can turn into a real crab, which is not your true nature.

Although you enjoy being with pleasant people, you need some time to yourself. It's a good idea to spend fifteen or twenty minutes alone each day in a peaceful place, to soothe your nerves and refresh your spirit. Your home should contain a special hideaway, where you can catch your breath and relax in peace when the stress becomes too severe.

Your ruler, the silvery moon, influences your interests, appearance, personality, sexuality, and emotional nature. Here are some examples of its effect on you:

- *Tender heart*
- *Soft curves*
- *Demanding side*
- *Sensitivity to criticism*
- *Love of home-cooked meals*
- *Excellence as a hostess*
- *Fondness for children*
- *Secret shyness*
- *Strong intuition*
- *Inability to forget old hurts*

Yours is a dynamic sun sign, which means you are active and eager to achieve. An instinct to protect is deep and basic to your nature. Security is very important to you, and that goes for both your emotional and monetary needs.

Any career you choose should offer a reliable income that fills your financial needs and makes you feel relatively secure inside yourself. Moon girls are versatile and have the ability to succeed in a vast variety of careers, from sales to medicine. Much depends upon your personal interests and ambitions.

Because you are exceptionally caring, you may choose a profession which involves seeing to the needs of others, such as nursing or child care. Other career possibilities that suit Cancer's nurturing nature are cook, dietitian, probation officer, restaurant management, nutritionist, health-care worker, physiotherapist, personnel work, museum curator, and of course, mother. The list is endless, and the choice must be your own.

74

Employers and co-workers appreciate your kind ways and caring concern for them, which becomes obvious when they are sick or feeling low. You work very hard when the situation requires extra effort, and you make an excellent executive.

Spending comes naturally to the average moon girl. You enjoy buying beautiful home accessories and provide well for your family. Many of you are avid collectors, who delight in searching through antique shops and garage sales, looking for treasures to add to a collection. Dolls and antique jewelry are popular collectibles.

A peek into your financial future reveals some great times ahead. When Jupiter, the planet of growth and abundance, moves into one of your horoscope's financial sectors, you can gain through wise investments or partnerships. So keep your eyes open for opportunities!

Careers to Consider

Certain careers are ideally suited to your sun sign. You may find success as a:

- *Diet consultant*
- *Advertising agent*
- *Caterer*
- *Health spa owner*
- *Silversmith*
- *Social worker*
- *Swimming pool designer*
- *Nurse*
- *Public relations agent*

With Friends and Family

Once you decide to accept a person into your inner circle, you are an excellent friend. You choose your companions carefully. Cancer's natural caution makes you want to be sure you have a good rapport with a person, before welcoming him or her into your life.

Your nurturing disposition can be a tremendous asset to your friends, but

protective or your friends may interpret your behavior as bossy or clinging.

Pets are popular with moon girls. You find it satisfying to nurture a puppy or kitten, and watch it mature into an adult animal.

Your sensitive and feeling nature attracts people who feel rejected or are in crisis

occasionally you can go too far. It's best to avoid projecting too strong a parental image. You like to take good care of your friends, but make sure your attentions are needed. Most adults don't want to be smothered by maternal behavior. Avoid being over-

The longer you have a pet, the more you enjoy the bond of understanding and communication that develops.

People of all ages enjoy spending time with you. You are excellent with children and seniors, as well as your own age group. Your sun sign group is very devoted to old pals, and often keeps in touch with aging relatives who live alone. You never neglect your near and dear (or even your dear and not-so-near).

Male friends find you helpful and appreciate your little kindnesses. Many men enjoy being mothered a bit, as long as it doesn't come with a sense of guilt or inadequacy. Female friends admire your ability to make everyone feel comfortable in your home. Your sensitive and feeling nature attracts people who feel rejected or are in the middle of a crisis. You provide a sympathetic ear and a shoulder to cry on.

Moon girls are creative, and many get satisfaction from making little gifts for friends. You may be one of those Cancer angels who make cookies or afghans for friends (or baby-sit for their children). Few signs

of the zodiac are as generous as you, loving Cancer.

Best Traits

- Emotionally responsive
- Loyal and patient
- Sympathetic
- Nurturing
- Creative

Worst Traits

- Tight with money
- Extremely touchy
- Possessive in friendship
- Moody
- Live in the past

ROMANTIC *Profile*

ment. Breakups can be very difficul[t] for you, especially if you are the injured party. You never forget an emotional slight—real or imagined.

Romance can be tricky for the Crab: one step forward, one step back. Sometimes you put up an almos[t]

Your celestial ruler, the silvery moon, has given you powerful emotions that dominate your love life. Your shifting desires and needs can be hard for a partner to predict. This presents a real challenge for some lovers. You'd be wise to find a mate who can sense (and happily live with) your frequently fluctuating moods.

Date to die for:
romantic moonlit walk on a deserted beach, with frequent pauses for kisses

impenetrable wall, which prevents smooth emotional communication.

There's a shy quality behind your lovely smile. You like to think you're totally independent (and you can be, when necessary), but you really want someone special by your side. That means you should probably take your time about marriage or long-term romantic commit-

Simple pleasures are a joy for you. You get a kick out of exploring antique shops and model homes. You like lingering over long, leisurely meals with your lover. You may even do the cooking once in a while. (Let him do the cleaning up!)

Your sun sign is inextricably linked to the element of water. You enjoy vacations near the sea or a picturesque lake.

SPECIAL RENDEZVOUS
In the butler's pantry of a Gothic mansion

Your Ascendant Reveals How Others See You

Second in importance to your sun sign, your rising sign determines the image you project. The inner you may be different, but your ascendant guides your automatic reactions to situations.

Aries: bold, impulsive, assertive, independent

Taurus: loyal, stubborn, patient, reliable

Gemini: witty, restless, versatile, talkative

Cancer: moody, cautious, vulnerable, intuitive

Leo: proud, ambitious, passionate, luxury-loving

Virgo: critical, practical, methodical, hardworking

Libra: tactful, refined, intelligent, charming

Scorpio: shrewd, intense, powerful, secretive

Sagittarius: open, restless, cheerful, curious

Capricorn: steady, honest, practical, authoritative

Aquarius: unique, friendly, stubborn, inventive

Pisces: kind, sensitive, adaptable, spiritual

(See Instant Ascendant Locator, p. 252, to locate your rising sign.)

Significant
Others

There is no "bad" sun sign for romantic Crab girls. But when it comes to building a lasting relationship together, some signs suit better than others. Any match can work if *both partners are willing to work at it.*

Your Best Bets

An alliance with another **Cancer** brings deep understanding and at least some degree of compatibility. Your mood swings may cause some clashes, but at least you'll understand where each other is coming from. You'll eat lots of good meals together.

Libra is attentive, but your mood swings upset the peace. He wants to please you, but sometimes that's a giant task. Try to work with him and relax a bit; this can be a winner.

Taurus brings stability and satisfies your need for security. If he's a typical Bull, you can depend upon him when things are rough… and he can say the same about you. You're good for each other.

Pisces is sensitive, mysterious, emotional…a worthy outlet for your caring nature. If you can find each other in the mist, this can be an exciting love match.

Scorpio is deep, loyal and security-conscious. You have passionate times together. If you respect his feelings and sometimes let him feel dominant, it can work.

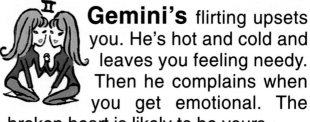

Gemini's flirting upsets you. He's hot and cold and leaves you feeling needy. Then he complains when you get emotional. The broken heart is likely to be yours.

Capricorn offers the security you want. You can give him the warmth and devotion he needs. An unusually compatible pair.

Worst Prospects

Leo feels strangled by your super-sensitive feelings. You find him aloof, bossy, a show-off. Not much to work with here.

Aquarius wants wings; you want an anchor. You yearn for undying devotion; he plans to stay free. Not recommended.

Virgo wants everything to be perfect. Your shifting emotions rattle his nerves. The way he picks on you hurts your feelings. Hard as you try, he never seems to be happy.

Your gentleness appeals to **Aries;** you'd stand by him through tough times. But would he stay with you? Don't bet on it.

Sagittarius wants a brief fling; you want a life-long partnership. Don't settle; it's not worth it!

Passionate
Interests

Women born under the influence of Cancer are highly creative. Hobbies abound, and practically everything you make can become a conversation piece. Decorating and entertaining come naturally to moon girls.

Chances are, you collect something, maybe without being aware of the habit. It may be cookbooks, earrings, salt and pepper shakers. It may be beaux; moon girls are popular with the opposite sex. Antiques are popular with Cancerians. You appreciate the history and enduring beauty of fine old furniture, jewelry and artwork.

Music that soothes and inspires suits you; your nerves fray easily, and you find comfort and renewal in harmonic sounds. As sensitive and talented as you are, it's natural that you enjoy the best creations of past and contemporary artists. Paintings by Monet and Manet typify styles of artwork that please your tastes.

Travel satisfies your need for an occasional escape. Your watery element beckons: cruising and seaside vacations are high on the list of preferences. Even at home you like to feel close to the sea. You may enjoy an aquarium, sea shells, or pictures of seascapes in your home or office.

82

You'd get satisfaction from exploring Hawaii, the Bahamas or San Francisco. Venice is another fabulous "great escape." You're surrounded by water and lovely old buildings (and don't forget those handsome Italian males, with their flashing eyes and beguiling smiles!).

Water sports are naturally appealing—and a great way to tone and firm a shapely Cancerian's body. Swimming, water skiing, and scuba diving are fun. You'd enjoy fishing with a rugged lumberjack in the Canadian woods.

Cancer girls tend to be patriotic. A perfect charitable outlet for you is visiting patients in veterans' hospitals.

It's heartwarming...and some Moon Girls have found love in this unusual setting.

Romance novels and waltzes are perfect for your leisure hours. They suit your romantic nature and inspire delightful dreams!

Happiest When...
- with your favorite relatives
- new curtains grace your windows
- your cooking is praised
- the kitchen smells good
- a guest brings a house gift

Wouldn't Be Caught Dead...
- burning your bra
- letting anyone know you're envious
- at a prizefight
- spelunking
- dirty dancing at a dive

Domestic Style

toes that remind you of good times and precious relationships.

Home is where you go when you want to escape the bustle and stress of the outside world. You feel safe there and do as you please. Some signs choose showplaces to live in to draw attention to themselves. Your home is private: a protective shell, inside which you can flop in a big soft chair and unwind. Comfort is the operative word for you.

For you to feel cozy in your home, its furnishings must reflect your interests and put you in a cheerful mood. You surround yourself with things that have special meaning for you. Photographs of loved ones stand on the furniture; more are tucked safely in a drawer. You treasure these souvenirs from the past. It may get a bit cluttered, but you don't mind. It's hard to part with memen-

Entertaining is not done lightly at your home, for it reveals your personal side. You want guests to be at ease. Even though it involves a lot of work, it's a pleasure for you to

have loved ones eat at your home on holidays. When special events occur, you go "all out." You never forget the little touches that make friends feel welcome—pretty candles, cloth napkins, lovely china and crystal and, of course, tasty food. You try to make at least some of the delicacies yourself, and order the rest from a good caterer or market.

Some daughters of the moon like being with people most of the time; others prefer more time alone. In any case, you need *some* quiet time to settle your sensitive nerves and refresh your spirit. Solitude has different meanings for different people. Find a peaceful place that offers the privacy you need to meditate, read, make plans or just be silent. An attic may suit your purpose, especially if it has the antiques you enjoy. Its remoteness is a comfort. Add a touch of silver to your private retreat; silver is Cancer's power metal.

The Cancer Cook

The kitchen is one of your favorite rooms, which isn't surprising, as the Moon, your ruler, represents the comforts of home. You are an imaginative cook, often concocting meals without the aid of a recipe. You love the task of entertaining on the holidays: you'll spend hours planning and weeks preparing for these special occasions. You always remember who likes what, and make sure they get it. No wonder people ask for your secret recipes!

Ten Years From Now...

Most moon girls will have spent some happy times away from home. Your major wanderings may be over, but you have the videos of your trip to Venice or exotic Algiers, where you met that mysteriously alluring stranger. It's hard to believe you really did venture so far—but you'll never regret it.

Although you still feel young, and look even younger, you are gathering what you call your "rocking chair memories": those mental souvenirs of romantic adventures and loves so sweet, though never meant to last, will keep you warm as you sit by your fireside in the years to come.

You've probably broken at least one heart; many men form almost dependent attachments to Cancer women, and it's hard to let go. Your soft heart bled for your suitor, but you couldn't act against your heart.

Chances are you've reached a position of respect in your profession, rejecting more than one marriage proposal along the way. The right proposal came at last, though, and you're settling in. Now you're ready to try a new career for size—possibly one where you can work from home.

Will you find fulfillment as a doting wife and working mother? It all depends on your partner. You need a mate who's loyal, supportive, has a sense of humor...and is an expert diaper changer. With your nurturing tendencies, you're probably inclined just to do it all yourself...but don't! If he hasn't yet learned to pull his weight in the nursery, now's the time to teach him!

After all, you can't be expected to run the city's best catering service and also take care of the twins you're expecting. In any case, you need a partner parent, and most men can learn!

You have an astonishing capacity to give, and you still haven't quite learned not to overdo it. Keep working at it. When you do, life will be much smoother!

Potential Pitfalls

Here are a few dangerous tendencies you should work to avoid:

- Being obsessed with anything
- Living life through others
- Staying in a dead-end job
- Clinging to relationships that are over
- Marrying just for financial security
- Fearing things you shouldn't
- Trying to control people by making them feel guilty
- Taking love for granted
- Being stingy
- Worrying about your weight

Regal Leo lady, you were born when the sun was in the part of the sky ruled by the constellation of the Lion. That gives you the distinction of having the sun as your planetary ruler. Our sun is actually a star named Sol, and you are truly the star of the zodiac family. Sol's child is proud, noble, powerful, and dignified—a born leader.

The Zodiac is an imaginary band across the sky that divides it into twelve zones. Each zone is ruled by a different constellation. Your horoscope is a chart showing the positions of the celestial bodies when you entered the world. It's true that to know *all* your secrets, we'd need a complete map of the sky, showing the moon, Mercury, Venus and the other planets in the positions they held at your birth. (The human body is seventy percent water, so all exert a subtle "tidal" pull on us.) But the sun, as the strongest force in the solar system and the dominant factor in the horoscope, determines a majority of our traits and inclinations. That doesn't mean you can't change them: you are free to handle these inherent tendencies as you choose. You may embrace, reject, or modify them to fit your unique sense of self.

Tradition has assigned each sun sign a gender, quality and element, based on its position in the zodiac. Leo is a *masculine* sign, made of *fixed fire.* The masculine designation refers to your active (as opposed to receptive) approach to life. Fixed means you are steady, persevering, and strong-willed. Fire reflects your blazing spirit, which can warm or inflame others.

Leo's symbol is the Lion, which explains your regal nature and authoritative manner. You feel special and expect others to recognize that fact. You want the very best of everything.

Your ruler, the sun, has given you warmth, vitality, enthusiasm, and creativity. Just as Sol is the center of our solar system, you flourish at the center of attention.

Your Profile:

Resonant colors: Gold, orange
Stones: Ruby, cat's eye
Plants: Marigold, tamarind
Day: Sunday
Number: 1
Parts of anatomy: Heart, spine, eyes

Confident Leo ladies love to be seen, heard and admired, for you are the royalty of the zodiac. Your dramatic personality and natural warmth set you apart from—and in truth, above—less spectacular types. You need a kingdom of your own, large or small, where you can reign supreme.

Being a proud lioness, you do everything in a big way. Even if your wallet's anemic, you'd much rather have a capuccino in a five-star hotel than a multi-course meal in a cheap bistro. What's more, you don't confine your lavish treatment to yourself only. You are very generous and want people to appreciate your open-handedness. You want to get as much out of life as you can. If this means stretching yourself thin, you still manage to have more fun—and accomplish more—than most.

Passion and enthusiasm are prominent in your fiery nature. Though ambitious in your own right, your real strength lies in your ability to inspire *others* to great achievements. You are a natural leader with excellent managerial skills. Co-workers and friends automatically latch onto your goals and strive for them. You can also inspire passion: your smoldering sensuality attracts many secret admirers.

True, you can be bossy at times. You know you could organize other people's lives much better than they do themselves...and given half a chance, you will. Leos make wonderful pals, partners and parents, but they often expect too much from their loved ones. If this sounds like you, maybe you should back off a little and get in touch with your pussycat side.

Instead of being demanding, you might encourage your friends and loved ones to develop their *own* interests. Nagging tends to put people on the defensive. Self-motivation is more effective than pressure from an outside source, however well-intentioned.

Sol, source of life, endows you with creativity in many forms. You can turn an ordinary evening into a festival, and a simple meal into a feast. But it's in the boudoir that your flair for fun is most exciting. There the mighty Lioness turns into a tantalizing tigress!

Admirable Traits
- Fearless
- Noble
- Self- confident
- Loyal
- Generous
- Sensuous
- Passionate
- Impressive

Aggravating Traits
- Vain
- Stubborn
- Domineering
- Indulgent

THE OUTER YOU

ure, career and personality. Cultivate it. Your clothes are well-made and always classy. Anything you wear looks fit for a queen; you insist on it and you're right. It's not in your nature to compromise on quality.

Although a female Lion doesn't have the mane of a male, your hair deserves its share of attention. Most lionesses prefer a loose, natural looking style. Just don't let it get so out of control that it ends up looking messy. If you wear your locks loose, don't forget to brush them often to keep them shiny.

As important as the sun is to the solar system, so is your heart to your

Natural charm, a friendly disposition, and a glowing personality give you lifelong youthfulness. You have a dramatic air that declares, "I'm special!" And so you are.

> *Your clothes are well-made and always classy. Anything you wear looks fit for a queen...*

You have a flair for choosing the perfect outfit and look to suit your fig-

body. The heart is the body's life sustaining force, and is traditionally associated with Leo. Aerobic exercise is important for you: it strengthens the heart muscle and keeps the blood circulating through your entire body as well. Like love, exercise puts a youthful glow on your cheeks. Good eating habits are also essential. Pay special attention to heart-conscious diet advice, and stay away from rich fats and salt.

Leo also rules the eyes. Take good care of yours. Sol's daughters are naturally sun-worshippers, so don't forget to wear good sunglasses to protect your eyes from damaging (and wrinkle-causing) rays. And don't neglect them with the make-up. A hint of shadow can make a dramatic difference!

Leo girls have a feline grace when walking, moving lithely on strong, well-proportioned legs. It's worth spending a little extra time to keep your legs firm and beautiful. And always pay special attention to your posture and carriage. Pull back those proud shoulders, and lead with your pelvis on every stride. You should look like a royal personage as you strut down the street. Broadcast the confidence you feel. It's a jungle out there...but you're the queen!

You're a real powerhouse of a girl, thanks to the influence of the sun, your sign's ruler. It shows in your appearance, interests, personality, and inclinations. Here are some ways the sun affects you:

- *Magnetic good looks*
- *Creativity in all sectors*
- *Champagne-and-caviar tastes*
- *Loyalty to loved ones*
- *Taking on tasks others fear*
- *Fun-loving nature*
- *Impressive personality*
- *Generosity (maybe too much)*
- *Desire for the best*
- *"Big thinker"*

Leo is the classiest sign of them all. You look like a million bucks even in the simplest suit. And you don't skimp on your wardrobe... or anything else. Spending comes naturally to the big-hearted Leo girl. You enjoy having the best, and you're willing to pay for quality and beauty, whether purchasing a home, a car, or a gift for your lover. When you're out shopping for a dress, you just naturally gravitate toward the highest priced designer labels.

Somehow you always seem to have the resources you need to live a comfortable life. You can be quite generous and live lavishly when you have plenty, but you don't need millions, because you instinctively handle money well.

Associates and co-workers appreciate your generosity of spirit, which is most apparent when someone is sick or has a personal problem. You always pitch in to make life simpler for them. That doesn't mean you're a weak leader;

far from it! You're a strong manager with high standards, and you expect subordinates and fellow executives to abide by them.

Few careers aren't suited to your wide range of abilities and interests. The entertainment industry and the political arena are ideal choices for a confident Lioness. You are happiest when you achieve something that you've had to work hard for. Whether your choice is classical ballet or heading a corporation, you perform your job with panache and more than a little drama.

A peek into your financial future indicates you can achieve some exciting gains in the next few years. If you are in a family business or a business partnership, you may want to consider expanding into broader markets.

Careers to Consider

Certain careers are ideally suited to your Sun Sign. You may find success as a:

- *Florist*
- *Theatrical agent*
- *Entertainer*
- *Child care worker*
- *Diamond dealer*
- *Politician*
- *Government official*
- *Resort director*
- *Photographer*
- *Dramatist*

With Friends and Family

The Lioness is a proud, self-sufficient animal, who seldom asks for assistance. You don't need people, but that doesn't mean you don't enjoy being with them. You have a wide circle of acquaintances, but probably only two or three very close friends.

Tenderness and warmth flow from you freely, along with advice on how

Many Leos have at least one pet, to whom they are devoted. Beautiful collies and fluffy Persian cats are favorites for Leo. Could it be because of their lush, mane-like coats? Or perhaps it's their dignified and regal air.

You enjoy companions of all ages, but seniors and youngsters find you especially appealing

to do everything better. Your advice is usually good, though it's not always wanted. You enjoy companions of all types and ages, but seniors and youngsters find you especially appealing, probably because you sincerely care about them.

You enjoy occasionally throwing a sumptuous party at your home. You invite friends and business acquaintances, and go all out to impress them with your taste and lavish style. Going stag is not for you. At all social events, you like to have an attractive

96

admirer on your arm—or in your regal entourage.

You seldom discuss your personal affairs with outsiders. Serious family problems are kept within the home. Diplomacy is not your strongest point, so you need to make a special effort to be tactful at social occasions. There's a time and place for confrontation, and a party isn't it.

In friendships, you expect to be the dominant force, and almost always are. Some men have been known to misinterpret your strength of character as passion for them, or your natural warmth as seductive tactics. But you're not one to play games. You soon set straight any man who makes an inappropriate move.

Female friends find it difficult (or downright impossible) to compete with your sensuous good looks and your ease with the opposite sex. You may want to lower the heat, if you notice a friend raising an eyebrow at a party. Then again, maybe not.

Best Traits

- Magnanimous
- Honorable
- Warm and loving
- Fair-minded and forgiving
- Good at organizing activities

Worst Traits

- Demanding, dictatorial nature
- Rigid opinions
- Tendency to show off
- Arrogant
- Spend-thrift tendency

ROMANTIC *PROFILE*

Loving you is like living beside a volcano. Your partner never knows when you're going to erupt--and when you do, things get *very* hot.

You attract admirers the way flame attracts moths, and you expect to be in control. If you feel you're in danger of being dominated by a lover, you become uneasy. Your partner needs to watch his step. He can rarely upstage you without getting into trouble.

You love the thrill of the chase. The majestic Lioness stalks and catches her prey, then does what she wants with it. But the Pussycat side of your nature also needs harmony in personal life. The hunt is one thing; warfare is another.

When you find the love of your life you show him off. Trouble is, you ge jealous if another woman pays too much attention to this paragon

When your emotions are engaged you are quite vulnerable, so be carefu not to display your prize too proudly.

Although you may not let your love know it, you control most romantic situations. Your passion simmers when your mate is open about his desire

You are instantly turned off by a partner who fails to respect you. And a partner who cheats on you gets no second chance!

Once you've selected a mate, you can be stubborn about keeping him, even if he proves a disappointment. Some Leos even hide their true nature to please their partner. But you needn't play a role to attract lasting love. Just be your lovable self. You deserve the best.

Your Ascendant Reveals How Others See You

Second in importance to your sun sign, your rising sign determines the image you project. The inner you may be different, but your ascendant guides your automatic reactions to situations.

Aries: bold, impulsive, assertive, independent

Taurus: loyal, stubborn, patient, reliable

Gemini: witty, restless, versatile, talkative

Cancer: moody, cautious, vulnerable, intuitive

Leo: proud, ambitious, passionate, luxury-loving

Virgo: critical, practical, methodical, hardworking

Libra: tactful, refined, intelligent, charming

Scorpio: shrewd, intense, powerful, secretive

Sagittarius: open, restless, cheerful, curious

Capricorn: steady, honest, practical, authoritative

Aquarius: unique, friendly, stubborn, inventive

Pisces: kind, sensitive, adaptable, spiritual

(See Instant Ascendant Locator, p. 252, to locate your rising sign.)

Significant Others

There is no "bad" sun sign for regal Lionesses. But when it comes to building a lasting relationship, some signs suit better than others. Any match can succeed *if both partners are willing to work at it.*

Your Best Bets

Living with another **Leo** produces either love or hate. You are quite well-matched sexually, and agree on the need to live in luxury. You can reign together in harmony, if you can avoid trying to rule each other.

Aries brings passion, excitement and novelty to a partnership. He's strong and passionate, just the right type to tame a lioness. He's one of the few people who can get away with telling you what to do—once in a while.

Libra is attentive and wants to please you. You can show off this elegant partner at social events and enjoy good sex at home. But beware: he doesn't enjoy competition.

Sagittarius is a rover and an adventurer. You like his wit and optimistic outlook on life; he likes your generosity and passion. Just beware of your jealous streak.

Scorpio is intense and exciting. He reciprocates your loyalty, but is dominant in subtle ways. This steamy love match can succeed, if both work at it.

Aquarius impresses you through logic and with his eccentric ways. He is dazzled by your poise and magnetism. The physical attraction may not be powerful, but cerebral pleasures will compensate, if you let them.

Worst Prospects

Gemini gets bored if you aren't at least as amusing as he is—not that you can't be, but it's exhausting. The physical part may be worth it for a while, but this match is hard to sustain.

Cancer's clinging ways stifle you and take the fun out of life. He's as super-sensitive as an exposed nerve, and the lioness has no taste for pussy-footing.

Virgo is a nag. You want to be queen in your home, but he points out your every shortcoming. Conflicts galore.

Capricorn is ambitious and image-conscious. You are a lovely accessory— but are you willing to be just that? If he's sensitive, it may work. But if he's a workaholic, you'll feel neglected and rejected.

Taurus is attracted by your strong sexual magnetism. You'll exhaust him, if you're an ambitious woman.

Pisces promises undying love. But be skeptical. Next week you may catch him kissing the girl next door.

Passionate Interests

Leos love to travel...especially first class (or on a private jet). As a daughter of the sun, you try to extend the summer by taking the most luxurious vacation you can afford. Whatever the season, you usually prefer warm climates with good opportunities to model your sexy swimsuit.

You like to go places where you can rub shoulders with celebrities, and where there are plenty of bright activities after sundown. Some Leos enjoy gambling in flashy casinos. You can not only show off your glamorous new clothes, but maybe even hit a jackpot! If you swim, it's likely to be a quick dip, then back to shore or poolside to flirt with those tanned musclemen. They can't take their eyes off you!

You adore being pampered for a few weeks at one of the plush spas nestled in the Arizona desert. Massages, facials, pedicures, manicures and aromatherapy are so relaxing and satisfying. You come out feeling as glamorous as a movie star.

For a change of pace, try a romantic weekend in St. Moritz. There's plenty of sun on the slopes, and you'd look fabulous in a gold turtleneck and black ski pants. Besides, you may meet Liz or Ivana on the way home. The Concorde lounge is as good as any beach resort for celebrity-gazing.

You are as generous with others as you are with yourself. You probably support several charities. Anything that benefits needy children appeals to your giving nature.

Your reading list may feature romantic novels—particularly those about a girl's rise from poverty to riches. Biographies of the rich and famous inspire and amuse you. Both provide vicarious satisfaction for your love of luxury.

You choose music to suit your mood at the moment. Even your favorite artist won't appeal if the song doesn't reflect your feeling. When you're feeling sexy, you may select rock or Ravel's 'Bolero.' When you're feeling blue, nothing can turn on the tears like a weepy country-western ballad.

Happiest When...
- you know you look fabulous
- flattered by someone you admire
- your taste in clothes is praised
- invited to an elegant place
- your lover gives you an expensive gift

Wouldn't Be Caught Dead...
- admitting your ring is a CZ
- sitting alone in a corner at a party
- at a wrestling match
- watching a Beverly Hillbillies marathon
- as a heavy metal (or any other) groupie

Domestic Style

You take care to ensure that your home represents you and your values. You decorate it in a style that reflects your warm personality and your excellent taste. Leo women see themselves as head of the household, and expect those who share their home to treat it—and them—with respect.

Sol's daughters like rich woods, earth colors, and bright rooms. Lots of light is a must, but give careful thought to the placement of lamps. Not everyone wants to sit in strong light. Invest in dimmer switches so you can control any glare.

The lion's den is full of activity. At times your home may resemble a circus with pets, friends, children and activity all over the place. But in general, you have control of your environment, and you maintain at least a semblance of order.

Entertaining, for you, can be either a joy or a strategy. Most of

your gatherings are rather casual, designed merely to get loved ones together. But you can manage a polished social function when your goal is to impress new acquaintances or business associates. Whatever the occasion, you serve exquisite foods and beverages. You are a creative hostess, often serving fancy treats such as imported coffees and dessert chocolates. Parties at your home are memorable for excellent cuisine and delightful company. Nothing but the best is served to your guests!

With your hectic schedule, you need a private den or hideaway, where you can withdraw for much-needed time alone. When it's not needed as a private retreat, you may use your den for sewing, hobbies, or reading.

Lionesses love nature—especially when there's sun to bask in. A yard or garden can be a delightful retreat, in any season. A lawn chair or a gazebo transforms an ordinary backyard into a haven. Whether the area is abloom with flowers or sparkled by snow, it's an inviting place to meditate or think out problems.

The Leo Cook

You are generous and loving, and you show it through the sumptuous meals you serve to friends and family. You can cook, but won't do it if you'd have to rush. If you do have time, fantastic desserts are your specialty. You are an alchemist with chocolate and liqueurs, and your sumptuous sweets are often works of art, with a painted plate or lacy praline garnish.

Ten Years From Now...

Pesky relatives kept asking, "When are you going to settle down?" "When I'm ready," you'd reply. Until recently, you weren't even ready to consider making a serious long-term commitment. You were having too much fun exploring your talents and the world!

But you have no regrets now about bidding adieu to your wandering ways. Whether it was a farewell tour as the Bolshoi's prima ballerina or a big send-off from your London firm, you were ready when the time came to make a career move. Many invitations tempted you (one to play Titania with the Royal Shakespeare Company was hard to resist), but you'd already decided to return home for a bit of "normal" life. Glamour is second nature to you, but that doesn't mean you don't get homesick.

By now, you've made so many romantic conquests, you've lost track of the number. Glamorous men gravitated to you; you've probably rejected a high-profile financier, or maybe a prince. The years have treated you kindly, and your suitors are no fewer, only more mature. That's probably why, after much careful looking, you've finally found a mate who's at ease with your strength. So far, you're both quite comfortable in your roomy Tudor mansion, and you see no reason to expect less in the future.

Your opportunities for achievement seem to increase as each week passes. You've had your choice of careers, and are happily established in a high-class, high-profile social set.

So here you are, perhaps bouncing

a baby on your lap, while chairing the latest fundraiser for the children's hospital. The RSC may have gone by the boards, but you're considering local options. Meanwhile, you're content rehearsing your lines for the community theater's production of Blithe Spirit. You're also the only mom in the neighborhood who spends vacations scaling the Matterhorn.

It's no wonder your friends are jealous. Their husbands all say you look decades younger than they do! A proud Leo isn't about to let a little thing like time wrinkle her brow!

Potential Pitfalls

Here are a few dangerous tendencies you should work to avoid:

- Becoming a snob
- Being domineering with loved ones
- Acting like an alley cat
- Showing off your designer labels
- Gold-digging
- Designers who experiment with sleazy fads
- Infidelity in a "monogamous" relationship
- Falling for insincere flattery
- Overdramatizing things
- Hogging the spotlight

How clever of you to be born while the sun was in the sign of Virgo—famous for intelligence and good taste. As a result, you are modest, practical, industrious and discriminating. You enjoy learning new things and analyzing people and situations. Virgos tend to be logical, orderly, and skeptical.

The zodiac divides the sky into twelve zones, each dominated by a constellation. To know all your secrets, we'd need a complete natal chart showing the moon, Mercury, Venus, and the other planets in the exact positions they held at your birth. All exert a subtle "tidal" pull on us, for the human body is seventy percent water. The sun is the dominant factor in the horoscope. As the strongest force in the solar system, it determines the majority of our characteristics. That's not to say you're stuck with all these traits. The natural inclinations are there, but it's up to you to embrace or resist them as you choose.

According to its placement on the zodiac wheel, each Sun Sign has a gender, quality, and element, which describe its essential nature. Virgo is a feminine sign, made of mutable earth. Feminine refers to your receptive (as opposed to active) approach to life. Mutable means you are versatile and adapt to various circumstances. Earth makes you reliable, cautious, practical, and hardworking. People depend on you in all aspects of your life, and they are seldom disappointed.

Virgo's symbol, the Wheat Gatherer, is depicted as a young virgin. She represents the modest and industrious nature of those born under this sun sign.

Your planetary ruler, Mercury, endows you with a keen mind, which can detect even the tiniest flaw or fallacy. Because you are very alert, you tend to be nervous and restless. The positive sides of these traits are adaptability and a tremendous drive to succeed!

Your Profile:

Resonant colors: Navy blue, dove gray
Stone: Sapphire
Plants: Morning glory, sage, blackberry
Day: Wednesday
Numbers: 4, 5
Parts of anatomy: Intestines, nervous system

Creativity and adaptability are just two of your many virtues. Virgo girls tend to be shrewd and rather reserved. Mercury, the mental planet, is your ruler. Firmly grounded in reality, you usually choose to follow the most sensible course in life.

You have a keen mind and approach everything from an analytical angle. Being an intellectual sometimes makes you feel alone, isolated from people who aren't as bright. Your brain is often miles ahead of your companions', and it's frustrating for you when they can't keep up. But your agile mind can open many doors. Use it to your advantage.

You are the queen of cool. When faced with a serious problem, you remain rational and never panic. You personify grace under pressure. Your level head is admired by everyone who sees you in action. A natural survivor, you exude competence.

You take great pride in doing your duty. Virgos are dependable friends, workers and mothers. But you're not emotionally demonstrative. It's easier for you to show respect for a friend than to be openly affectionate. Although you're not given to physical displays of emotion, that doesn't mean you don't care a lot.

In romantic relationships, you are strong, independent and unpredictable. You are surprisingly earthy in your lovemaking. You give thought to what will make you happy and how to acheive it. For this reason, Virgos often marry later than some sun signs.

You are detail-minded and see everything. You have a knack for making the most scattered bits of information come together to make sense. This makes you ideal for many professions. But this same trait makes you hard to live with. You call attention to others' shortcomings. No one loves a critic—especially an accurate one. The truth hurts!

Your amazing powers of discrimination make you want everything "just so." This is an admirable goal, but unrealistic. Your perfectionism can cause endless worry and frazzle your nerves. And your aura of dissatisfaction rubs off on everyone around you. Perfection is a fine goal, but you can't really expect to meet it. If you could just accept yourself and others as is, life would be so much nicer.

Admirable Traits
- Versatile
- Practical
- Efficient
- Unselfish
- Judges by results

Aggravating Traits
- Nervous
- Critical
- Inquisitive
- A worrier

THE OUTER YOU

you don't like it. Just remember: it's the truth that hurts. Next time a friend makes a suggestion, consider taking it for a change.

Mercury girls often play down their looks. Your type of natural beauty stands out in classic career clothes—think Katherine Hepburn in *Desk Set*. Shoulder pads in structured jackets and blouses are a must. They make you look authoritative, and they slim your waist. Update your image by getting an easy-care hairstyle.

Virgo girls are big on fitness, diets and nutrition. You eat, breathe, sleep, and discuss health. In fact, the typical Virgo is a bit of a closet hypochondri-

Your best physical features are your hands, bone structure, and engaging smile. Wise Virgos women take good

> *Your type of natural beauty stands out in classic career clothes...*

ac. You're gung ho and also a little bit touchy on the subject. It's fine for you to criticize your health habits, but if anyone else points out deficiencies,

care of these assets. Make sure you take time for dental hygiene, and use hand cream several times a day. (Keep a small jar handy—in your gym bag or desk drawer.)

Sleep is very important to your sense of well-being. You work hard, so be sure to always get enough sleep to feel rejuvenated by morning. On those rare occasions when you overdo partying, vitamin C and lots of water will purify your system.

You'd enjoy and benefit greatly from gentle yoga postures that slowly release tension, while stretching away muscle tightness. Gardening is a good way for an earthy Virgo to stay in shape. Aerobic dancing and fast walking are other possibilities.

Although you look professional in office knits, tweeds and suedes, be bold when a special evening is on your calendar. Select a sheer lace gown in your favorite shade of blue, from icy to indigo. Dare to wear glamour that glimmers. Sequins are scintillating by candlelight.

Mercury, your sign's planetary ruler, influences your attitudes, interests, personality, and love nature. Here are some ways Mercury affects you:

- *Mentally alert*
- *Youthful at any age*
- *Eager to learn*
- *Curious about many things*
- *Never sit still for long*
- *Attracted to bright men*
- *Quick to sense trouble*
- *Can do two things at once*
- *Know things others don't*

Your Career/Cash

It's a lucky boss who has you on her team. You take pride in your product, and you never shirk a duty. Mercury, your special planet, gives you an ability to coordinate mental and physical activity. Your mutable sign makes you highly adaptable and a whiz at communication. In discussions and presentations, you carefully choose the exact word that conveys your meaning. You are a shining example of the conscientious and dependable craftswoman.

Career options abound for the clever Virgo lady. Your penchant for detail lets you shine in a job that involves collecting and analyzing apparently unrelated details. Your mind runs like a high-powered computer, bringing order to chaos.

Your kind of skills are a precious commodity in modern business. There's a demand for medical technologists and librarians who have

your insight, vision, and eye for detail. Clerical workers in doctors' offices, hospitals and other medical facilities are at a premium. You may find a dietician's work to your liking.

Accounting, tax law, and computer repair are ideal fields for your special abilities.

Your helpful nature makes you popular on the job. You're always on the ball when the schedule is tight, or someone is out due to illness. You catch co-workers' errors. You seldom make mistakes, so your own work doesn't need redoing. Your financial habits veer toward caution. Whether you're choosing a car, an apartment, or a designer suit, you weigh the advantages and disadvantages, then make an educated choice.

During the next few years, Jupiter, Uranus and Neptune spark many important changes in your lifestyle, position, and earning ability. You are being readied for bigger and better things. Your financial future looks golden.

Careers to Consider

Certain careers are ideally suited to your sun sign. You may enjoy working as a:

- *Nutritionist*
- *Animal trainer*
- *Accountant*
- *Interpreter*
- *Scientist*
- *Statistician*
- *Psychiatrist*
- *Efficiency expert*
- *Data analyst*

With Friends and Family

Making your friends happy is a primary pleasure for Mercury girls. You work hard to nurture cherished relationships. Don't go too far: sometimes you are so busy seeing to friends' physical comfort, you forget to sit down and relax for a good chat. Your kindness is appreciated, but instead of fussing over whether a friend's tea is warm enough, give her kind to anyone who's sick or depressed. You can be a good listener, but be careful not to do too much talking. Sometimes a chum just needs you to hear out her tale of sorrow.

...you can probably count your true friends on the fingers of one hand.

a chance to help you occasionally. Friendship is a two-way street, and she knows it. No need to stagger through a house move without asking her to help pack boxes.

You get along well with people because you're considerate. You are

Active people and achievers fascinate you. You admire their energy, and you're curious about how they achieved their success. You may want to see if you could follow their example, and accomplish more.

You have a large circle of acquaintance, through work and other activities. You take the trouble to stay in touch, so your relationships have staying power. Still, you can probably count your true friends on the fingers of one hand. These are the people who'd bail you out of jail at 3 a.m. on a rainy night, without asking any embarrassing questions. Once in a while, someone you thought you could count on disappoints you by not being there when you need her. But that's rare, for you are a good judge of people.

Men like the fact that you can be a platonic pal, with no ties or role-playing at all. You see men as equals, and as a result, they regard you the same way. When you get together with friends, your main interest is stimulating conversation. Any other amusement is strictly secondary.

Best Traits

- Honest and modest
- Keep commitments
- Enjoy helping friends
- Intelligent
- Good listener

Worst Traits

- Worry, worry, worry
- Fussy about small things
- Inquisitive
- Nervous and restless
- Harsh and judgmental

ROMANTIC *Profile*

You like to make love in a crispy clea[n] setting. For you, there's no romance i[n] rumpled sheets and pillows strew[n] around the room. To explore you[r]

Mercury girls are not effusive or sultry by nature. Your warmth takes the form of kindness, and thoughtfulness, and true caring. Thinking about your sweetheart sets you aglow with love, but not ablaze with uncontrollable lust. You have set emotional and physical boundaries that you seldom cross. To lovers, you are generous and considerate, but never a doormat.

romantic nature. become more at eas[e] with the physical side of love. You[']ll never be an all-night carouser. and re[al] promiscuity is not your style, so it's oka[y] to let yourself go a little. You'd love a g[ift] of your favorite scent, the one too price[y] to buy yourself.

Your early upbringing may have taught you to repress sexual desires. Once you let your feelings surface, you discover you enjoy making love and being in touch with your sexual side. You come to understand that love belongs in everyday life—not tucked away in a secret rose-scented drawer.

Your analytical nature may lead you to dwell on a lover's shortcomings. It's not a bad idea to explore what works and doesn't work for you, but be careful not to offer criticism while you're in bed. Minor problems should be discussed at a neutral time, without placing blame. You could spend less time analyzing your emotions and more time exploring and enjoying your basic earthy sensuality.

*Special Rendezvous:
In a penthouse suite in a
five-star luxury hotel*

Your Ascendant Reveals How Others See You

Second in importance to your sun sign, your rising sign determines the image you project. The inner you may be different, but your ascendant guides your automatic reactions to situations.

Aries: bold, impulsive, assertive, independent

Taurus: loyal, stubborn, patient, reliable

Gemini: witty, restless, versatile, talkative

Cancer: moody, cautious, vulnerable, intuitive

Leo: proud, ambitious, passionate, luxury-loving

Virgo: critical, practical, methodical, hardworking

Libra: tactful, refined, intelligent, charming

Scorpio: shrewd, intense, powerful, secretive

Sagittarius: open, restless, cheerful, curious

Capricorn: steady, honest, practical, authoritative

Aquarius: unique, friendly, stubborn, inventive

Pisces: kind, sensitive, adaptable, spiritual

(See Instant Ascendant Locator, p. 252, to locate your rising sign.)

Significant Others

There is no "bad" sun sign for Mercury's practical daughter. But when it comes to building a lasting relationship, some signs suit your needs better than others. Any match can succeed *if both partners are willing to work at it.*

Your Best Bets

Romance with another **Virgo** means life is orderly. Both value work and judge by results. There's not much surprise or spontaneity, but you do understand each other.

Cancer does a good job of courting you. He makes you feel loved, and you make him feel appreciated. This pairing can work, if you avoid excessive nitpicking.

Partnership with a **Taurus** brings stability and a satisfying love life. He's stubborn; you're adaptable— an ideal combination, but make sure you don't cave in too often, or you'll start to feel put-upon.

Capricorn is a likely partner. Strong, dignified, and earthy in romance, he values your high standards and knows how important a career can be.

Restless **Gemini** is drawn to your warmth and caring ways. If you are self-sufficient and have a full life without him, this may work.

Pisces is shy and sensitive. If you are gentle with him, he may fill some of your hidden needs. But you have to open up and let him in.

Worst Prospects

Scorpio is looking for emotional intensity; you don't have it. You get nervous when his mood darkens. His possessive nature will stifle you.

Aquarius is too cool for you; you need someone to ignite the emotional spark. And his behavior is erratic; better look for someone you can count on.

Sagittarius is a bachelor at heart. He likes the comforts you supply, but won't reciprocate. If you're not careful, he'll convert your considerate ways into something like servitude. Besides, his flirting with other people makes you uneasy.

Leo is at the mercy of his heart. You are ruled by reason and logic. Neither really understands the other.

Aries wants immediate gratification, but he may lose interest after he gets it. You are willing to wait for something meaningful—and lasting.

Libra wants to please his partner. He needs your approval. Your tendency to criticize will quickly wear him down.

Your personal planet, Mercury, has given you an active and agile mind. You have a wide variety of interests and pursue them to the limit, often becoming an expert in those that most fascinate you. They may include anything from architecture to zoology—and almost always a craze for the latest diets and health issues.

Even when you're not really trying, you're constantly learning new things. Art and literature appeal to you as ways to continue educating yourself. Museums provide the peace and beauty you need after a demanding work day. They're also great places to meet interesting men.

Wheat Gatherers are more intellectual than athletic. Baseball or tennis may appeal to you, but prob-ably only as a spectator. You are also drawn to dance, with its fascinating precision of movement and the beauty of its music.

Giving to charity comes naturally to you. You support a favorite cause. Chances are, you have collected funds or done other volunteer work.

Travel appeals to you, but only on your terms; you insist on a good price and exactly the right accommodations. You occasionally experiment with new places, sampling their exotic foods and customs, but generally you prefer to stay with the tried and true. Once a place strikes your fancy, you'll keep coming back. You like to know what to expect when you visit a different town or order a meal in a restaurant. You'd rather not travel alone, preferring to share the experience with your family or a friend.

You're such a hard worker, you really deserve a wonderful vacation. Consider making a great escape to the Swiss Alps. You'll love the fantastic mountain views and the crisp clean air. Who knows? You may even learn to yodel, or bring

a gorgeous ski instructor home with you as a lifelong souvenir.

Happiest When...
- you can answer all the Jeopardy questions
- a lover gets everything right
- your crystal stemware gleams
- your work wins an award
- life goes according to plan

Wouldn't Be Caught Dead...
- at a wrestling match
- writing in a library book
- vacationing at a dude ranch
- with grease under your fingernails
- sleeping on dirty sheets

Domestic Style

You know it takes more than pleasant surroundings to make a happy home. Your home life, whether you live alone or with someone, is the base that supports all the other parts of your life. You want a haven, where you feel safe and unconditionally loved. Your home reflects your tastes, values, and personality.

The ideal dwelling for you has attractive lines and a quiet but beautiful interior. You enjoy a garden or being able to see greenery around your home. Needs change, so you are likely to move several times before settling in for the long term.

You enjoy creating a comfortable home, but you're too busy to have time for daily dusting. Nevertheless, you keep things in order; you can be a fanatic about organizing closet and shelf space. You alone are in charge of your household, and you can become fretful if your domestic routine is disturbed. Interfering friends or in-laws upset your delicate nervous system. Don't let resentment build.

Let them know right away if they're overstepping their bounds.

When you entertain, you tend to go all out, serving a delicious meal to your guests. The trouble is, you may get so frantic about details, you lose your pleasure in being a hostess. You are pleased if guests bring wine or a treat to eat. And you bless those who help you clean up after the festivities!

If you have children in your life, try not to be too critical. Correct them if they do something dangerous, but allow them some freedom to grow and explore, even if it means letting them make mistakes. No one benefits from having every tiny flaw pointed out, especially at an early age.

You need some time to yourself each day, to relax, read, or catch up on your correspondence. Find a quiet place where you can unkink your nerves. A garden bench or a study with a view of greenery is ideal for taking your mind off daily aggravations.

The Virgo Cook

If you're a typical Virgo, your kitchen is clean and organized, featuring an array of pots and pans designed for specific uses (woks, steamers, fondue pots). You work in a neat, orderly manner, cleaning as you go. You serve nutritious foods, since you're always aware of health needs. You enjoy making special treats for loved ones. (Your beau loves grapes? Serve him ham veronique.) Consider taking a course in gourmet cooking. You'll get an A+.

Everyone's always thought of you as modest and reserved, but time has mellowed you in many ways. If they'd seen you dancing on the table at the Club Rendezvous last night, they'd never have recognized you! Some liberating relationships—including that liaison with an Italian race car driver in Monte Carlo—have led you to kick up your stiletto heels to some different tunes.

You've found satisfying outlets for some, if not all, of your nervous energy, and you are learning to enjoy life. If your neighborhood didn't offer the kind of recreation you wanted, you probably launched it yourself. You may be leading a reading group or organizing house tours.

Your constant steady industry paved a straight and narrow road to success, but it gradually wore you down until you felt the need to escape.

Many Mercury girls take serious sabbaticals; you may have abandoned a job to live on a kibbutz or a lover to go study French (men) at the Sorbonne.

You're back by now, but surely not to the same old grind. You seem to become more mercurial each day, sweeping into the Main Street Library with an armful of computer software one day, and with a software company CEO on your arm the next. (You obviously know something other girls don't.)

Your kind heart has probably led you to at least one life-changing event. You may have decided to adopt a child (or two), or found a new career in advocacy...or perhaps you met your dream mate while serving as a volunteer fireman. (After you rescued him from an inferno and gave him the kiss of life, it's no wonder he fell in love with you!)

At this point, you're on the brink of a big decision. You probably have offers on several fronts: career, marriage, and maybe some exciting travel in the offing. Should you marry your hunk-in-distress or go for that work-study course on the animals of Antigua? The options aren't all compatible, but don't waste too much time fretting over your choice. They're all winners—how far wrong can you go?

Potential Pitfalls

Here are a few dangerous tendencies you should work to avoid:

- Becoming "Miss Prissy"
- Missing out on fun
- Lovers who won't commit
- Habitually overworking
- Focussing on flaws

- Thinking you know it all
- Taking friends for granted
- Scattering your energy too widely
- Ignoring spiritual needs

Take a bow, generous Libra! You deserve a medal for all the favors you've done for others through the years. Your strong sense of justice leads you to go out of your way for others. And because you value harmony highly, you have strong negotiating skills. You are also active, tactful, charming, and creative... no wonder you attract admirers as flowers attract bees.

The zodiac divides the sky into twelve zones, each governed by a different constellation. Your horoscope is a map of the sky at the time of your birth. To know *all* your secrets, we'd need a complete natal chart showing the moon and all the other planets in the positions they held at the moment you were born. All exert a "tidal" pull on us, for the human body is seventy percent

128

water. But the sun is the most powerful force in our solar system. As the dominant factor in the horoscope, it determines the majority of our characteristics. Free will lets you handle your traits and inclinations as you wish—you can accept, reject, or expand each as it suits your style and ambitions.

Tradition has assigned each sun sign a gender, quality, and element, which describe its essential nature. Libra is a *masculine* sign, denoting an active (as opposed to receptive) approach to life. Its *cardinal* quality means you excel at starting things, and are result-oriented. Your element is air: you have a fine mind and are more cerebral than emotional.

Libra's symbol is a Scale in perfect balance. It represents your quest for balance in your life, and your fondness for justice. You weigh both sides carefully before making any decision. You treat everyone as an equal, and expect similar treatment from them.

Venus is your ruling planet. Named for the goddess of love, it imparts grace, beauty, and a desire for harmony. Venus's daughters tend to have romantic natures and a desire to avoid confrontations.

Your Profile:

Resonant colors: Midnight blue, teal
Stones: Lapis, opal, carnelian
Plants: Jasmine, catnip, calendula
Day: Friday
Numbers: 6, 9
Parts of anatomy: Kidneys, lower back

Any person who wins your loyalty is lucky indeed. The sign of Libra produces some of the most fair-minded and appealing women in the zodiac family. You project an image of charm and elegance. Tact, social poise, and thoughtfulness are your birthright. Your consideration for others and your attunement to their needs make you a desirable friend and partner.

Venus's children have a reputation for being indecisive, but in fact, you make decisions with confidence. It's just that you take the time to weigh all aspects carefully before arriving at your decision. Those born under your sun sign have the ability to see all sides of an issue. That objectivity makes you an excellent source of feedback in private and professional life. You don't make split-second decisions; you always take your time. But once you've decided, you'll stick with your choice.

Libra is not only the sign of love and peace, but also of war. Fair and generous as you are, you also demand justice for yourself. You can only defer to others' needs for so long. If they make the mistake of over-stepping the limits of your generosity, they will see your fighting side—and it can be truly formidable. Your anger is all the more powerful because it's backed by reason: you are fighting for your legitimate rights. No one wants to be on the receiving end of your annihilating (verbal) wrath.

One of your main goals in life is to achieve and then maintain a sense of balance; no life sector should be neglected in favor of another. You are very conscious of conflicting needs and the duality of situations; you often feel as if you're being pulled in two directions at once. It's great to be broadminded, but it can cause tremendous stress if carried too far. Remember, you can't please all the people all of the time. You need to be flexible and master a give-and-take approach. If you can center yourself psychologically, you'll see yourself and others clearly, and be able to keep priorities in proper order. Don't forget yourself in your efforts to be fair to others. Once in a while, your needs have to come first.

Admirable Traits
- Promotes harmony
- Cooperative
- Diplomatic
- Charming
- Creative
- Fair

Aggravating Traits
- Aloof
- Changeable
- Interfering
- Avoids confrontation

You like to project a confiden image. Wear clothes that make yo look and feel like a winner. (On th rare occasions when you venture ou in sweats, you always end up regre ting it; you feel at a disadvantage you don't look your best.) And don neglect your face. Many Libra wome view makeup as frivolous—who ha the time? But you'd be amazed ho much *more* beautiful you can be wit some simple additions. Powde cream foundation can highlight th delicate glow of the Libran comple ion. Even a perfect rose looks bette in the right vase.

The typical Libra lady is elegant, charming and refined. Outstanding

> *Many Libra women view makeup as frivolous—who has the time?*

features are your fine skin, lovely smile and the shape of your face. Somewhere you have at least one dimple; it's a Libra trademark.

Your sign's ideal colors are deep but not bright: midnight blue, tea dark fuchsia, and other intense tone that attract attention without scream ing for it. Your goal should be t enhance *you,* not to make your *outfit* memorable. Understated elegance fits your classic good looks.

Venus's daughters tend to be gracefully curvy. You'll never achieve that waif look, but nobody wants you to. If you think your curves are getting out of control, avoid rich sauces, heavy meals and alcoholic drinks. (Liquor is *loaded* with calories.)

To most Libras, exercise comes under the heading of work, not recreation. But even if you loathe the very word *exercise,* you need it. That doesn't have to mean hours of sweat at the gym. Take the trouble to find a way to make exercise appealing. Walking with a partner or a pet is pleasant, and it tones vulnerable hips and thighs.

You're a thinker and often can't turn off your thoughts at bedtime. Try heading for bed half an hour early, to give your mind time to clear itself. You need proper rest to do your work, and to deal with all the important issues you face every day.

Venus, your sun sign ruler, affects your interests, appearance, personality, and approach to everyday life. Here are some examples of its influence:

- *Attractive at any age*
- *Appreciate beauty*
- *Enjoy socializing*
- *Deeply passionate*
- *Loving partner*
- *Fun to be with*
- *Drawn to quiet places*
- *Enjoy art and music*
- *Born romantic*

Libra lasses have the rare ability to relate to all classes and types of people at a moment's notice. This unusual quality makes you ideally suited for working with people. You shine in jobs where you bring beauty, comfort or harmony into others' lives.

Many actors, models, writers, designers and commercial photographers are Libras. Artistic ability is in your nature. Whether it's a talent for music, writing, painting, sewing, or giving parties, you have a creative side that you should nurture and develop. If you don't earn money through your talent, you can still use it to get more joy from life. Your sense of balance and justice serves you well in many careers. Ideal choices include lawyer, florist, beautician, diplomat, marriage counselor, bridal consultant, museum director....The list is varied and endless. You'd be wise to avoid dark and gloomy workplaces,

high-pressure positions, and jobs that require you to compete with other people. Your innate fairness inhibits your ability to push ahead of the competition.

Bosses and co-workers enjoy having you on their team. You're willing to work long hours when required, and you are a very fair-

minded girl. You firmly believe in equality for all, and you live up to that splendid ideal.

To you, money is a tool for enjoyment. You put some savings aside, but the future never takes precedence over the present joy of owning lovely things. It's important to you to wear attractive clothing and to live in a pleasant place. After all, your ruler is Venus, goddess of beauty.

During the next few years, you take a much more creative approach to increasing your income. Jupiter and Uranus open new doors to you, which had been previously shut. You have unexpected breaks and amazing opportunities to express yourself in ways that make money. You are given new and important assignments, that improve and strengthen your position in the workforce.

Be prepared for positive action, savvy Libra lady!

Careers to Consider

Certain careers are ideally suited to your sun sign. You may find success as a:

- *Marriage counselor*
- *Bridal consultant*
- *Author of fiction*
- *Diplomat*
- *Public relations agent*
- *Lawyer*
- *Jewelry designer*
- *Diamond merchant*
- *Musician*
- *Human resources director*

With Friends and Family

Handsome men with strong personalities and a luxurious lifestyle are your favorite friends. Not that you don't enjoy being with other girls...you do! But you sometimes sense envy coming from women who aren't as attractive or appealing as you.

You're an expert at honest flattery and turning on the charm. Sincere compliments glide through your luscious lips. You wrote the book on how to win friends and influence people—without even thinking about it!

You see friends as a source of entertainment and, when necessary, emotional support. Chances are, there's one really close pal whose loyalty you cherish. You avoid social relationships that take lots of work or commitment. You're too busy with your personal life to look elsewhere for heavy responsibilities.

You are never bored in the company of your friends. They make you feel good about yourself.

Amusing, clever people appeal to you: you are never bored in the company of your friends. They stimulate you mentally and make you feel good about yourself. You *like* people of all ages and backgrounds. But because you are a full-time thinker, you spend much of your time with people who share your interests or admire your abilities.

You do your best to be friends with your siblings and other close relatives. Pettiness is not in your repertoire, and there's nothing to be gained by feuding with people you're going to be forced to spend time with. You go out of your way to maintain good relations, and if things go wrong, you keep working to improve the situation.

A pet may play an important role in your life, not only as a companion, but as an object of beauty. You prefer animals who are attractive and easy to live with. (You may enjoy the sleekness, loyalty and exclusivity of a sable Burmese cat—there are only 5,000 in the U.S.) If you're a dog lover, a regal Afghan or Borzoi would suit your elegant taste.

Best Traits

- Friendly, outgoing
- Considerate and cooperative
- Charming, easygoing
- Intelligent communicator
- Appreciative

Worst Traits

- Moody, sometimes to extremes
- Exacting about details
- Indecisive
- Impatient
- Emotionally aloof

ROMANTIC *Profile*

You are a romantic with a capital R. You love flowers, moonlight, candlelight suppers, blazing fireplaces and close dancing in the dark. You have an ideal love nature. Not only are you gentle, affectionate, fair-minded and highly attractive, but you adore the fun of a romantic chase and an old-fashioned courtship. The man who wins your love is lucky: your main goal is to please him.

It's only natural for you to look your best for your lover, dressed or not. You make your partner's life and his home a thing of beauty and a joy forever. When it's your turn to make the advances, you pour on all your charm and elegant sensuality.

The only problem is, darling Libra girl, you *hate* being lonely, and you need a partner's approval. Your yearning for love, combined with your giving approach to romance, can leave you wide open to disappointments. Nothing turns you off

> ### *Date to die for:*
> *Champagne and seduction at a Parisian sidewalk cafe*

more than a mate who's disloyal or not attuned to your superb sensitivities. When you find a mate who is as loving and thoughtful as you are, your heart will sing.

You're almost always looking for a lasting relationship; you'd love to settle down with a life partner any time he appears. But you're so much in love with love, you can easily be talked into linking up with someone who has no designs on your future. There's not much point, for you, in the romance of the moment. You'll be happier once you've learned to say "no" when someone wants *you* to do something you don't want.

Special Rendezvous:
Tango dancing till dawn in a
candle-lit ballroom

Your Ascendant Reveals How Others See You

Second in importance to your sun sign, your rising sign determines the image you project. The inner you may be different, but your ascendant guides your automatic reactions to situations.

Aries: bold, impulsive, assertive, independent

Taurus: loyal, stubborn, patient, reliable

Gemini: witty, restless, versatile, talkative

Cancer: moody, cautious, vulnerable, intuitive

Leo: proud, ambitious, passionate, luxury-loving

Virgo: critical, practical, methodical, hardworking

Libra: tactful, refined, intelligent, charming

Scorpio: shrewd, intense, powerful, secretive

Sagittarius: open, restless, cheerful, curious

Capricorn: steady, honest, practical, authoritative

Aquarius: unique, friendly, stubborn, inventive

Pisces: kind, sensitive, adaptable, spiritual

(See Instant Ascendant Locator, near back of book, to locate your rising sign.)

Significant Others

There is no "bad" sun Sign for loving Libra ladies. But when it comes to building a lasting relationship together, some signs suit your needs better than others. If you love someone whose sign is hard to live with, the match can work *if both partners really work at it.*

Your Best Bets

A love match with another **Libra** is sure to be pleasant. The only question is, who'll make the first move? No problem: just take turns.

Gemini is drawn by your charm and gracious manner. You find him amusing. The match may lack fire, but it's mentally stimulating. The danger is, he's as flirtatious as you, and he may not be in it for the future.

Life with **Taurus** brings stability, comfort and earthy sensual pleasures. You both appreciate beauty, and will share a harmonious home life.

Pisces is deep, mysterious, emotional. You are thoughtful and intelligent. Together you can create some fabulous fantasies.

Aquarius has never met a woman so lovely and easy to get along with. You've never met a man so crazy. If you stay open to his unorthodox approach, this can be a fun match.

Leo wants a consort to shower with love and reign beside him. You're willing and oh-so-able! You'll love doing everything together— right up to shopping for a ring!

Worst Prospects

Scorpio is too independent to understand your occasional need to rely on others. He's not interested in sharing all you want to share.

Aries' assertiveness is foreign to your nature and will clash with your sense of justice. If you really love him, be prepared to deal with his temper and selfishness.

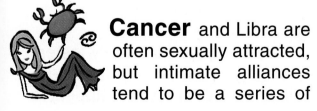

Cancer and Libra are often sexually attracted, but intimate alliances tend to be a series of conflicts. He's too possessive. You're loyal, but don't want to be smothered.

Capricorn is drawn by your charm and refinement; concern about public image makes him seek a mate who'll make a favorable impression. But he may demand too much; his notions of propriety can stifle your enthusiasm.

Virgo likes your vivacity and appreciation of beauty, but his frequent nagging is exhausting. You do want to please your mate, but with him, it seems impossible. You invite trouble, if you accept him as a partner.

Sagittarius is full of fun, but he lacks the sensitivity and consideration you deserve. He's the outdoorsy type; your inclination for elegance will intimidate him, and his fondness for physical activity will bore you. The fun wears off fast.

141

You put a high value on leisure time, and resent it when an overwhelming share of work interferes with outside pleasures. You put a lot of time and energy into doing things for other people. So, when your work is done, you're ready to kick off your shoes, put up your feet, and hang out a "do not disturb" sign.

Few sports appeal to Libra girls. You prefer to give your mind a work-out. You'd much rather read a spicy novel or phone a friend. You enjoy *watching* figure skating, horse racing and gymnastics for their beauty, but you seldom actually play any really active sport. If you had to pick a favorite outlet for energy, an evening of lively dancing with a favorite part-ner would win hands down.

You are generous with charities,

as in other things. You often donate money or clothing. Your sense of fairness demands that you share with those less fortunate than you. But taking part in marches or marathons to raise funds is simply not your style. You're more likely to work with a program for reading for the blind. That personal contact is so much more rewarding!

Many Libra women enjoy doing beautiful craftwork—making pil-lows, creating floral arrangements, embroidering or designing clothes is both fun and satisfying for you.

Your fondness for beauty fosters a strong interest in fine art. Paintings and sculptures appeal to you; you could spend all day in one tiny gallery if you had time. If you're a true Libra, your nose is often buried in a book. You may have favorites that you reread from time to time. If you haven't read *Gone With the Wind* and *Rebecca,* you have two big treats in store. They're *your* kind of love story.

Travel is not essential for its own sake, but you do enjoy the occasional "great escape" to someplace really special. You might consider an early autumn trip to the Lake District in merry old England, or a New England B and B if you want to stay closer to home. A week of gorgeous scenery and gracious living will put you in seventh heaven.

Happiest When...

♎ playing an inspired game of Scrabble
♎ your lover brings your favorite perfume
♎ reading an intense love letter
♎ you look great without trying
♎ relatives get along well

Wouldn't Be Caught Dead...

♎ at a Grateful Dead Concert
♎ working out at dawn in sweats
♎ on an Outward Bound expedition
♎ without a comb
♎ leading a protest rally

Domestic Style

You're a whiz at turning the simplest house or apartment into an inviting and attractive home. You love a place that's airy and bright, elegant but not showy. You like to live where you can meet and spend time with smart, entertaining, lively people.

Housework is a dirty word to you, so you choose furniture that doesn't need much polishing or waxing. Simple styles are dressed up with carefully-selected accessories: attractive lamps, wall hangings, clocks, curtains...nothing in your home is merely functional. You like flowers and trees in your yard—preferably perennials that come back with no fuss—but somebody else had better do the mowing and weeding.

The most important feature of your home is a happy family (or anyone else you live with). You *loathe* confrontation. If people argue around you, it drives you crazy. Loud noise makes you cringe. Your radio is tuned to the mellow music station— good for relaxation, but no use for drowning out unpleasant noise.

Venus gives you your love of beauty and comfort. When you come home from a hectic day, you like to kick off your shoes and unwind in style. Your decorating scheme probably includes loads of luxurious throw pillows. Velvet-covered rockers and recliners are your favorite chairs.

Even if you're comfortable working in a bustling office (many Libras aren't), you need a quiet place to be alone when you get home. It takes you a while to release all that stress. You'll be a better companion to your partner if you first get some time to unwind.

Entertaining friends at home is something you enjoy, but don't do very often. It's too much work! You can't bring yourself to do anything halfway. When you have people over, you really do things right—candles, crystal, silverware, the whole shebang. Your parties are remembered

for being special, and you love that. Every hostess should be so lucky!

The Libra Cook

You bring thought and order to the kitchen. You incorporate appealing flavors, colors, and textures of foods. (A meal that's all one color disgusts you.) You can make a simple meal a triumph, but prefer to offer something fancy to guests. Refined manners and natural charm make you a perfect hostess. Your elegant meals are planned well in advance. When dinner guests arrive, they see a table set with fine china and gleaming crystal. When you're dining alone with your partner, things are less formal, but always delicious.

Ten Years From Now...

Your prudent outlook has served you well, and at this point in your life, you're thinking BIG. Your dreams for the future are broad and full of scope. You have a position of respect in your area of special interest, whether it's law, diplomacy, or floral design. Libra writers have seen their work in print, and love that by-line! Diplomats are being considered for positions in Paris (or is it Rio?). Lawyers are angling for a seat on the bench...unless you prefer to become a trial lawyer or a high-priced jury consultant. Of course, you'll review all possible life paths before making your next important career decision; a Libran wouldn't have it any other way.

You may not have found your ideal romantic partner yet, but you've had a lot of fun looking. You have a knack for discovering love in rich or exotic settings. (Memories of a certain balmy midnight in Morocco bring a rosy glow to your silken cheeks. How many people have experienced a tryst in a Maharajah's tent?) You love variety! But at this point, you're thinking less of the backdrop than of the ideal leading man.

After all your varied adventures, will you finally be ready to settle down? If you aren't in a committed romantic partnership yet, the time may be right to make a match. Your man of the moment could easily become the man of your life. (Or you may be just about to meet a prospect. Be alert to new acquaintances in the workplace and out.) You need a playful intellectual, who amuses and stimulates you. But before taking any vows, check his history with the opposite sex, employers and the bank. Your ideal mate supports you emotionally and financially, *and* is your mental equal.

Some Libra women would simply rather be on their own. If you value your freedom above all, your opportunities will arise in non-romantic areas. You may develop a new hobby or discover a perfect reading club. Whatever you choose to pursue, with your glorious smile, thoughtful manner and intelligence, nothing can hold you back!

P o t e n t i a l   P i t f a l l s

Here are a few dangerous tendencies you should work to avoid:

- Getting in the middle of a family feud
- Always deferring to others
- Men who don't treat you as an equal
- Dwelling on self-pity
- Setting your goals too low
- Thinking in happily-ever-after terms
- Trying to please everyone
- Settling for second best in men
- Being a couch potato
- Selling your creative talent short

Lucky you! You were born when the Sun was in the part of the sky ruled by the constellation of Scorpio. You are a woman of power, intensity and resourcefulness. You feel things deeply, but usually keep your feelings to yourself. Your penetrating gaze searches for hidden motives in those you meet. You *never* forget a kindness or a slight.

The zodiac divides the sky into twelve zones, each dominated by a constellation. Your horoscope is a map of the sky at the moment you were born. To get a complete portrait of the inner you, we'd need a full natal horoscope with the Moon, Mercury, Venus, and other planets in the positions they held at your birth. (The human body is 70 percent water, so they all exert a subtle tidal pull on us.) The Sun, as the

148

strongest force in the solar system and the dominant factor in the horoscope, determines most of our characteristics. But that doesn't mean you're stuck with all of them. It's up to you to handle each trait as you choose — accepting, rejecting or adapting it to suit your unique style.

Tradition has assigned each sign a gender, quality and element. Scorpio is a *feminine* sign, composed of *fixed water.* Feminine sun signs have a receptive approach to life. The fixed quality means you are persistent and firm-willed, and water signifies the depth of your feelings. *Fixed* water is ice—a potent force (don't forget, an iceberg sank the *Titanic).*

Scorpio has three separate symbols. The most familiar of these, the Scorpion, represents your ability to sting enemies. The Eagle embodies your ability to reach great heights through personal achievements. And the Phoenix symbolizes your ability

to start fresh after the most serious setbacks.

Pluto is your planetary ruler. Named for the god of the underworld, it gives you tremendous resilience, a sense of purpose, and the sturdy spirit that makes you a born survivor. You are a *powerhouse!*

Your Profile:

Resonant color: Burgundy, claret, maroon
Stone: Topaz, malachite
Plant: Chrysanthemum, ginger
Day: Tuesday
Number: 2, 4, 6
Part of anatomy: Pelvis

149

Scorpio's three symbols are unique in the zodiac —and the triple powers of regeneration, achievement, and a dangerous sting are unique in the human race. What an arsenal! Pluto girls are gifted with *enormous* potential.

No other Sun sign has anything near your inner strength. Your intensity is so strong, it sometimes scares timid souls. But you can look cool, even when seething with rage inside. The person who deliberately provokes your anger must be a fool or a masochist. You have a tremendous memory for good turns *and* bad.

Your charisma gives you an edge in the competition for love and jobs. Devotion to a principle can spur you to heroic actions. When you want something, you go after it, whether it's a relationship, a job, or a table at a chic restaurant. Because you go all out, you are likely to experience both the heights of happiness and the depths of despair.

You are loyal and loving in friendship and romance, and expect others to treat you the same way. When betrayed, you feel a deep desire for vengeance—and it may take years, but you'll get it. You can be ruthless, if you think a situation calls for it.

That's not to say you're generally destructive. Your mission in life is healing—even if it requires slash-and-burn measures to root out the problem. Pluto endows energy that purges, purifies and intensifies. It drives you to acknowledge any guilt or resentment you're harboring, then find ways to eradicate it. The Phoenix in you is all for starting anew, but first the old must be cleared away. Your deep feelings make you vulnerable, but they also enable you to live life more fully than other signs. Everything is more vivid to you, and more satisfying.

Admirable Traits
- Brave
- Shrewd
- Loyal
- Intense
- Powerful
- Magnetic
- Resourceful

Aggravating Traits
- Jealous
- Possessive
- Ruthless
- Calculating
- Vindictive

THE OUTER YOU

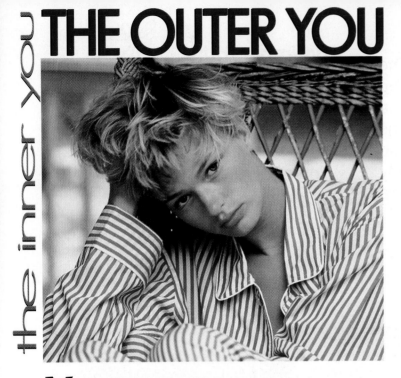

ic V-shaped Widow's Peak is the sp cial beauty mark of Scorpio.)

Scorpio girls never have that mas produced, cookie cutter look. Let ot ers imitate the cutesy look of eve TV star. Your beauty is strikir because you look like no one els Your unique and charismatic loo stand out in any crowd: you're a tr individual.

For Scorpions, make-up should subtle and muted in the daytime, bc and sophisticated for evenings out.

Your rare brand of beauty does not rely on a perfect profile or cover-girl

> *Your beauty is striking because you look like no one else. You're a true individual.*

hair. Your personal magnetism exudes power and sensuality. Your outstanding features are a penetrating gaze, strong eyebrows, and graceful proportions. Many daughters of Pluto have a beautiful hairline. (The dramat-

Scarlet, burgundy and dark red a your power colors. You should ha at least one stunning outfit in one these elegant shades. You have a t ent for finding the perfect accessori to accentuate your sleekly chic suits. Belts, hats, gloves, scarves, and bold jewelry fit the confident image you project to the world.

Your body is uniquely attuned to your feelings, so extremes of emotions may affect your complexion or your eating habits. When you feel blue or betrayed, you probably tend to binge on comfort food. Try to maintain a balanced emotional outlook: you'll avoid many stomach upsets and have an easier time keeping your weight steady.

Foods rich in vitamins A and E are important for Scorpio women. To get your vitamins, your menu should include corn, peanuts, wheat germ, tomatoes, and yellow and green leafy vegetables.

Never neglect your rest. (Be sure your mattress and pillow support your head and spine properly.) Sleep refreshes your body and helps prevent stress. With your overworked emotions, you need a good night's rest on a regular basis. Besides, it's worth setting aside time for your sexy dreams (and realities), sensuous Scorpio girl!

Your sign's ruling planet, Pluto, influences your looks, interests, personality, sexuality, and emotional nature. Here are some examples of Pluto's effects on you:

- *Alluring appearance*
- *Jealous streak*
- *Sensitivity to criticism*
- *Intimidating persona*
- *Loyalty to friends*
- *Devotion to mate*
- *Lust for power*
- *Alertness*
- *Strong intuition*
- *Tendency to remember wrongs*

Pluto girls regard wealth and position as power—and you want it! The desire for complete control over your life drives you to succeed. Although your power may not be a secret to the world, any occupation you choose is likely to contain an element of danger, or be out of the public view.

Research scientist or undercover detective, you are an expert at uncovering secrets. You get a kick out of knowing things others don't; it makes you feel strong. You'd make an excellent spy, industrial or international. Your natural magnetism draws people to you, and you can manipulate them as you wish. And the danger appeals to both the Scorpion and the Phoenix in you.

Managers and co-workers admire your ability to stay focused on a project until it's done. Once

you've accepted an assignment, you persevere—regardless of any hardships. Tremendous powers of concentration enable you to visualize a goal and ignore distractions. Professions that suit your resourceful and persevering nature include banking, physics, insurance, inheritance law, nuclear science, and locating missing persons.

A comfortable income gives you a sense of security. You enjoy owning things that bring emotional satisfaction or make you look powerful. The image projected by a Porsche in your driveway appeals to you.

The financially savvy Scorpio woman puts her cash into investments or a Keough account. You need a monetary cushion to fall back on, in case of a recession or career slump.

Your values are in the process of changing. Pluto is in your financial sector. During the next few years, you get money in ways others wouldn't think of. Recycling may be somehow involved. You develop a new attitude toward possessions. Congratulations, smart Scorpio girl. You're putting priorities in proper order!

Careers to Consider

Certain careers are ideally suited to your sun sign. You may enjoy being a:

- *Private investigator*
- *Surgeon*
- *Vice squad detective*
- *Magician*
- *Psychologist*
- *Foreign agent*
- *Funeral director*
- *Pathologist*
- *Chemist*
- *Pharmacist*

With Friends and Family

Many potential friends are drawn to your magnetic personality and obvious power. You know lots of people you'd classify as acquaintances, but just a few really close friends. You want friendships that endure and are reliable.

You're cautious; you know you can't trust just anyone. You're a loyal friend who's there when needed. You expect that same loyalty. If you don't get it, a friend can become an enemy for life.

have unlisted telephone numbers, or use a post office box instead of a home address.

Chances are, there's someone you'd cross the street to avoid. When you end a relationship, you never look back; no amount of pleading can change your mind.

When you end a relationship, you never look back;
no amount of pleading can change your mind.

Privacy is important to you. You often enjoy being alone to do your own thing. Friends must accept this need with no complaints. Many Scorpios

Scorpio is the sign of extremes. You are a bundle of contradictions. Sometimes you need tons of emotional support from friends. Other times you just want to go off by yourself to brood. Friends have to tread lightly to find the right response mode.

Although you can enjoy friends of both sexes, most of your intimate pals are probably women. You like to be with people who are independent and smart. You get along with people of various ages. But unless they're your children, you'd rather not spend much time with youngsters. You hate to be caught off guard in social situations, and you may feel uneasy around people you consider smarter or much richer.

Friends appreciate the fact that you never forget a favor. Most Scorpios are in the habit of sending thoughtful thank-you notes for gifts or other kindnesses. This makes you really stand out above the crowd of insensitive people who take nice things for granted.

Best Traits

- devoted and caring
- inspiring companion
- excellent listener
- trustworthy
- heroic in emergencies

Worst Traits

- rebellious nature
- prone to sarcasm
- secretive and suspicious
- domineering tendencies
- vengeful toward those who cross you

ROMANTIC *Profile*

`'A`ll or nothing' is your approach to love. You like the breathless meetings, the fiery fights, and the even hotter making up. You want a one-woman guy who'll never cheat. Any man who tries to use you is brave and stupid.

You need a partner who's into adventure, so you can live out your wild fantasies together. You believe in enduring love, and you're willing to work to keep it fresh and romantic.

The path of love is seldom smooth, and it can be downright dangerous, if you give in to your explosive temper. Try not to be too stubborn. you want to hold a mate, deactiva that time bomb. Get more control ov your emotions. After a flaming battl give the relationship a chance to ris out of the ashes. Learn to talk out yo problems calmly. You'll avoid lots headaches.

> ## Date to die for:
> *dancing to a Dixieland jazz band in a smoky "dive"*

Physical attraction may cause yo to link up briefly with Mr. Wrong. B you'll recognize him soon enoug

You can't be expected to stay in love with anyone who's weak or silly, or doesn't take you seriously. You need a mate with a good mind and deep emotions. Another Scorpio may be a good choice for a lifetime relationship.

Your sharp mind, sexual magnetism and sultry good looks attract romance. You have so many admirers, you can hold out for the best, so never marry in a rush.

Special Rendezvous:
in the office, after hours

Your Ascendant Reveals How Others See You

Second in importance to your sun sign, your rising sign determines the image you project. The inner you may be different, but your ascendant guides your automatic reactions to situations.

Aries: bold, impulsive, assertive, independent

Taurus: loyal, stubborn, patient, reliable

Gemini: witty, restless, versatile, talkative

Cancer: moody, cautious, vulnerable, intuitive

Leo: proud, ambitious, passionate, luxury-loving

Virgo: critical, practical, methodical, hardworking

Libra: tactful, refined, intelligent, charming

Scorpio: shrewd, intense, powerful, secretive

Sagittarius: open, restless, cheerful, curious

Capricorn: steady, honest, practical, authoritative

Aquarius: unique, friendly, stubborn, inventive

Pisces: kind, sensitive, adaptable, spiritual

(See Instant Ascendant Locator, p. 252, to locate your rising sign.)

Significant Others

There is no "bad" Sun Sign for Pluto's magnetic girl. But when it comes to building a lasting relationship, some signs suit your needs better than others. Any match can succeed *if both partners are willing to work at it.*

Your Best Bets

An alliance with another **Scorpio** brings understanding and at least some degree of compatibility. You both value loyalty, privacy and security. But watch out for that sting; you need to deal openly with resentment.

Cancer is a possible partner. If you respect his feelings, he may let you control the relationship through gentle wiles. Could be a satisfying match.

Taurus brings loyalty, stability and sensitivity. If you require intense passion, it's probably not here. He may be able to cook, which would be a plus, since you don't on a regular basis.

Pisces is sensitive, imaginative, mysterious, but your intuition lets you see inside him. This can work, if you can stand the Fish's slippery ways. But you may have to sacrifice some coveted control.

Aries likes your passion and strength. You find him sexy. If you strengthen your relationship through shared interests, this can be an exciting match.

Capricorn offers the stability and material security you want. You can provide the warmth and loyalty he needs. A compatible couple, if he's not a workaholic. If he is try to cure him before giving up!

Worst Prospects

Aquarius demands complete freedom to do as he wishes. You seek someone who will be as loyal as you. This is not an easy partnership.

Gemini's flirting upsets you. He hates it when you get moody. A broken heart is likely to follow if you take him on. Guess whose!

Leo is intimidated by your obvious strength. He reacts by turning stubborn — but so are you. There's little chance for understanding here.

Virgo is mostly talk and little real action. Your intensity makes him edgy. You hate his nitpicking. You clash more than you cuddle, which is bad for your psyche.

Libra is sweet and appealing, but he's not willing to offer the total devotion you expect from your mate.

Sagittarius is looking for a brief fling. You prefer a lifelong partnership. Don't bother.

The unknown attracts you and piques your curiosity. You like gothic romances or good mystery stories. You spend a lot of time observing people and figuring out the hidden motives that drive them. Sometimes you do private research on a topic of personal interest. Magic and sleight of hand intrigue you. You'd love to be in on the magician's secrets.

You're loaded with creativity and find satisfaction in using your many talents. You like to be with people who are independent and smart. Drama and the theatrical world appeal to your deep emotions. You'd be good working in a community acting group, behind the scenes or as one of the principal performers.

When you travel, it's likely to be for business or educational purposes. On those rare occasions when you take a trip for pleasure, you like a hotel that offers privacy and personal security.

You often receive requests from charities, but you tend to ignore most. You are not a scattered philanthropist; you prefer to support one or two causes that have a special meaning for you.

You are a fan of dramatic art: Wyeth, Van Gogh, or El Greco...their intensity excites you. When you view a great artist's work, you try to figure out the story behind the painting. You're fascinated by the way the artist uses light and shadow.

Your taste in music is unpredictable. It might be anything from the Grateful Dead to Blues Traveler to Berlioz. You're an individualist in this area. In any case, you're passionate about your likes.

The next time you're in the mood for a great escape, grab your scuba gear and head for the Galapagos Islands in the South Pacific, where you can swim in a sparkling blue-green sea and take an underwater tour of some of the world's most amazing creatures. It should appeal to your interest in the unknown... and your urge to know more than the next person!

Happiest When...

- a rival fails miserably
- planning a surprise party
- with lover beside a blazing fireplace
- trying exotic foods
- winning someone over to your opinion

Wouldn't Be Caught Dead...

- taking back an unfaithful lover
- admitting you're jealous
- revealing your best friend's secrets
- in a croquet tournament
- playing Truth or Dare

Domestic Style

Home is your retreat from a dangerous world. You feel safe there and do as you please. Modern life seems so stressful to you at times, you almost hate to go out your front door. After spending a hard day in an unfriendly world, you like to know a snug haven awaits you at home.

The location of your home isn't as important to you as the things *inside* the home. You surround yourself with things that mean security to you. You're possessive about certain items that you think of as "MY things." Anyone you live with knows it's hands off these pieces.

Both the give-and-take of family life and the pleasures of being alone have their appeal for you. You like to use your time as you want. You enjoy being a loner when you want to be, and with a partner when you feel that need. The trick is to find a partner who'll let you have it both ways.

You prefer to live in a place that's impressive. Your home probably

includes a unique piece of furniture or a striking architectural feature. You like a place with some history behind it, such as a Victorian house. You're a bit of a hermit at heart, so privacy is important to you; huge picture windows are too revealing for your taste.

You insist on the freedom to be alone whenever you want. This is necessary so you can sort out your thoughts and your complicated feelings. You usually retreat to a bedroom, a bathroom, or a study for these sessions.

Entertaining, to you, means having a trusted friend or couple over for wine and cheese, or something super-simple to prepare. You do more listening than talking at such get-togethers.

You insist on the freedom to be alone whenever you want. This is necessary so you can sort out your thoughts and your complicated feelings. You usually

retreat to a bedroom, a bathroom, or a study for these sessions.

The Scorpio Cook

Cooking per se doesn't excite you, unless you're entertaining special friends or loved ones. You live on take-out most of the time, but when you invite guests to dine, you go all out. Guests are better off staying out of your kitchen; you like to surprise them with whatever treat you're making. You have at least one secret recipe which people rave about. (One Scorpio girl is famous for her Red Devil Cake: simply add one small bottle of red food coloring to any chocolate cake recipe.)

165

Ten Years From Now...

By this time, chances are you've acquired an adoring partner and possibly a darling little tyke, who calls you Supermom. Your career—whether espionage or chemistry—has had enough twists and turns to stay exciting, but now you may be ready to switch gears altogether. Motherhood is surprisingly rewarding; you never knew you'd slip so naturally into domestic bliss. But even your absorbing family hasn't quenched your Scorpion appetite for stimulation. You're still a human dynamo, known for your past achievements and hungry for more.

Your financial situation is fabulous. You've been smart *and* lucky—if you haven't won a few million in a lottery, some of your stocks soared through the roof. Now that you have the time and money to fulfill some fantasies, you can retire your satin trenchcoat and fedora,

and quit your career of intrigue. You'll always treasure the secret memories you leave with (a shady rendezvous on Waikiki, a brief acquaintance with a Tunisian belly dancer...). But it's time to move on. The question is, what will you find to do in its place?

Your marriage will probably require some extra attention somewhere along the line. Don't forget to detonate that temper, or you may not pull through. Stronger couples will weather the storm and become sturdier than ever.

Now's the time to think seriously of uses for your financial bounty. Reinvest some in blue chip stocks, by all means. But use the rest to launch some long-contemplated projects. You might finally go on that fascinating-sounding submarine cruise under the Pacific. Who knows! It could be the start of a new career! Or you could do something big for your favorite charity...start collecting Wyeth or Van Gogh...buy a new car and the home of your dreams. (Be sure to consult with family members; remember, it's their castle, too.) Whatever you choose, make it spectacular. There's no need to horde the loot anymore. You're past that point, and proud of it!

Potential Pitfalls

Here are a few dangerous tendencies you should work to avoid:

- Marrying for money only
- Preconceived notions about love
- Falling for weak men
- Bingeing on chocolate
- Resenting richer women

- Fear of growing older
- Trying to dominate loved ones
- Making a habit of overworking
- Drinking alone
- Taking friends for granted

Congratulations! You were born when the sun was in the zone of the sky governed by the constellation known as the Archer. That makes you a sun sign Sagittarius, a true celestial distinction.

The Archer endows you with a sense of adventure and a love of challenge—not to mention penetrating insight.

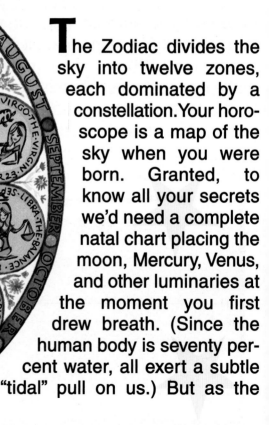

The Zodiac divides the sky into twelve zones, each dominated by a constellation. Your horoscope is a map of the sky when you were born. Granted, to know all your secrets we'd need a complete natal chart placing the moon, Mercury, Venus, and other luminaries at the moment you first drew breath. (Since the human body is seventy percent water, all exert a subtle "tidal" pull on us.) But as the most powerful force in our solar system, the sun is by far the dominant factor, determining some three out of four character traits. That's not to say you can't escape the negative ones—it's up to you to accept, reject, or adapt these tendencies to suit your unique style.

Depending on its placement in the wheel of the zodiac, each sign has a gender, quality and element expressing its essential nature. Sagittarius is a masculine sign, made of mutable fire. The masculine designation reflects your active (as opposed to receptive) style, while mutability confers flexibility, and the fire a flaming spirit that enables you to get others fired up (or steamed!).

Sag's symbol, the Centaur, stands for your complex dual nature: half human (read humanist, humane), half wild and irrepressibly untamed. Note the Centaur's bow and arrow; idealistic Archers aim high.

Your guiding planet is Jupiter, mythical ruler of the gods, and the zodiac's largest celestial body. A famously benign influence, Jupiter bestows expansiveness, a taste for exploration, and truly amazing luck, gifts that explain your sunny optimism and compulsion to push the envelope. (The mission of every Sagittarian is growth.)

Your Profile:

Resonant color: Purple
Plants: Carnation, birch
Parts of Anatomy: Hips, thighs
Stone: Turquoise
Day: Thursday
Lucky Number: 3

Charming, charismatic and more than just clever (Sag is the sign of the sage/philosopher), you're also a super conversationalist. Thanks to that zany sense of humor and insatiable zest for seeing and doing it all, you always have lots to talk about. No wonder hostesses line up with invitations, including some glamorous gatherings; wherever you wander, the zodiac's most cosmopolitan species fits right in.

Among your universally welcome traits: A firm belief in fellow earthlings—others sense and respond to your upbeat expectations. You are also beloved for a generous spirit that moves you to share possessions, paychecks, even past loves (you never were the clingy type!). Then there's that sterling integrity to recommend you. Friends can safely trust you with their money, man, life...so what if secrets are something else? Candor is your strong suit; discretion is not. You are refreshingly (sometimes painfully) honest. Just ask anyone who's ever solicited your opinion on a new heartthrob or hairdo only to get hit with a truth that stings. Dissembling is beyond your powers—and outside your interest. Ditto punctuality (too little time, too much to do).

But then, nobody's perfect, and you've never claimed to be. You may be impossibly gung-ho, when in the throes of a new craze (not everybody shares your enthusiasm for cyberspace). You're fiercely independent, a rebel in your teen years and commitment-shy forevermore. And occasionally, when feeling put upon, you can turn sarcastic (if only for a second and a half).

The funny part is, it almost doesn't matter how naughty you are. So pals do get exasperated with your unreliability now and then? Who could stay mad at a girl who so clearly means well, and is so sincerely high on them?

Admirable Traits
- Attractive
- Funny
- Creative
- Energetic

Aggravating Traits
- Impractical
- Fly-by-night
- Tactless
- Changeable

THE OUTER YOU

influence is the equine grace wit[h] which you move. Archers tend to b[e] long and leggy, with an angula[r] beauty that makes everything o[n] your back look like haute couture.

Shoot for clothes that play up you[r] sassy side—sexy safari suits, skin[-] tight bike shorts, a slit-to-here shi[rt] from that nifty shop in Chinatow[n.] Just so everything allows for eas[y] striding: Jupiter women hate to b[e] confined! The same goes for feelin[g] restricted to any one make-up styl[e.] Funky spiked hairstyles, daring blac[k] lipstick, deep blue nailpolish...all ar[e] fabulous looks for an experimente[r] who loves to turn heads. But no nee[d] to go overboard; you're just as fetch[-]

Twinkling eyes are your trademark—no matter what your build or bone structure, that Jovian taste for merriment and mischief gives you

Healthy, vibrant Sagittarians don't need much camouflage to shine.

away. That hint of fun attracts all sorts of admirers, and you never disappoint them. Another sign of Sag's

ing au naturel. Healthy, vibra[nt] Sagittarians don't need much camou[-] flage to shine.

172

Regimens too exhausting for others seem relaxing to you. Your best Rx for stress, in fact, is a strenuous workout—as long as it doesn't feel like work. You'll go all-out in the pursuit of adventure, or in the spirit of competition, and not even feel the pain. So get those endorphins coursing with some spirited horseback riding, rock climbing, deep sea diving... the more roaming and risk involved, the more fun you have. Do take care, though: Reckless Sag can be accident-prone.

One other caveat: at times you tend to overdo the eating, drinking, partying (blame Jupiter's profligate streak). Try to control that madcap spirit with a dose of moderation. You know there's nothing more tedious than a bad hangover—and you don't have time to waste a day sleeping it off! Archers also tend to suffer from problems involving the joints (Sagittarius governs the hips, thighs). Don't ignore warning signs, or they could get worse. Still, you're not about to be defeated by any silly old twinge. Centaurs have truly amazing recuperative powers, and one other enviable gift: whether 19 or 90, you never look your age!

Jupiter, your planetary ruler, endows you with certain traits—some good, some bad. Here's a sample:

- *Fun-loving*
- *Frank, sometimes to a fault*
- *"Big thinker"*
- *Optimistic*
- *Enjoys meeting new people*
- *Witty*
- *Willing to try new experiences*
- *Wastes time and energy*
- *Expansive*
- *Hates personal criticism*

Smart, versatile Archers can excel in virtually any field: your high energy and daring creativity can be applied to whatever you choose. You are especially suited for careers that offer challenging mental and/or physical stimulation, non-stop variety, lots of opportunity for crowd pleasing, and plenty of frequent flyer miles. You'd be a super foreign service attaché, politician, tennis champ, philosophy professor, traveling sales rep, or stand-up comedian.

Success usually comes quickly to Jupiter girls, thanks to your powerful intellect, knack for problem-solving (a unique mix of logic and creativity), and what critics call dumb luck. (Actually it has more to do with following your heart. Feminine intuition or full-fledged ESP, your hunches almost always pan out!)

The tough part is hanging in there when variety wanes. Dull routine can make you sick, which is why you're often happiest holding down two

jobs...less time for getting bored! You'd rather be exhausted than idle any day, and a good challenge can be stimulating. Just make sure you don't spread yourself too thin.

Whatever your profession (or professions), financial rewards are probably low on your list of driving factors. When an Archer talks about job benefits, she's usually referring to the freedom to steal a long weekend or the moral satisfaction of meaningful work, not a health plan or 40l(k). It's true that you'll never find contentment in monetary remuneration alone. But beware: scorn for salary can be a short-sighted policy for someone who's both devil-may-care and long-lived! Not that you should abandon personal goals to get rich quick, but you might consider some alternative saving strategies. Take that 40l(k): it could translate into a nifty little retirement villa in Spain. So, failing a regular company savings plan, why not have an investment specialist make periodic contribu-tions to a growth-oriented mutual fund? While you're at it, keep a big envelope handy for all those expense receipts that usually end up at the bottom of your knapsack; they could be deductible! And don't even consider doing taxes your-self...an IRS l040 may be the only foe that can faze Jupiter's daunt-less, detail-hating girl!

Careers to Consider

- *Teacher*
- *Safari guide*
- *Jockey*
- *Interpreter*
- *Missionary*
- *Bush pilot*
- *Physical education teacher*
- *Publicity agent*
- *Adventurer*

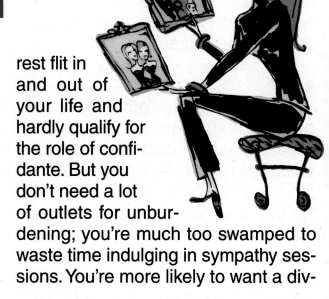

The zodiac's Pollyanna, you have a knack for bringing out the cheerful best in anyone who crosses your orbit. You exude goodwill and a sense of well-being, and it's contagious. Five minutes in your presence is enough to raise a companion's self-esteem. In fact, others actually become livelier and more lovable when you're around—and they sense it. So of course your rolodex is packed.

rest flit in and out of your life and hardly qualify for the role of confidante. But you don't need a lot of outlets for unburdening; you're much too swamped to waste time indulging in sympathy sessions. You're more likely to want a div-

Others actually become livelier and more lovable when you're around – So of course your rolodex is packed

The down side is that so few of those far-flung contacts know you really well. The Centaur girl spreads herself thin; the constant need for variety conflicts with any chance of having a regular crowd. Constant companions are limited to the select few who match the Archer's frisky style. The

ing buddy or someone to share a casual but stimulating chat over drinks.

A-list companions tend to be articulate fellow adventurers: a septuagenarian you met at photography class; a seven-year-old computer buff who's teaching you to hack; that sexy hunk who takes you fly fishing (Archers love being one of the boys). You're never less than lively company, so all will go out of their way to accommodate your busy schedule. Generally, though, you're a better fair- than foul-weather pal. It's not that you're not concerned, but Centaurs are too busy to provide a predictable shoulder to lean on. Besides, you make lousy camomile tea.

Even beloved relations know better than to expect a birthday card or help with blowing out the candles on the cake: you're both forgetful and habitually overbooked. Likewise, pets are cared for with maximum warmth but minimum fuss (get a self-sufficient cat, or a horse you can board). True, you'll go all out for the odd stray or lost soul, but only if you adopt them. You may be galvanized into action by outrage or plain old affection, but guilt and a sense of duty move you not one whit.

Still, admirers are willing to overlook your little lapses. Who else is so adorably tolerant of their flaws? Or so unfailingly amusing (provided they can catch up with you long enough to share a giggle.) Scintillating, scattered Archers invented quality time.

Best Traits

- Cheerful and optimistic
- Expansive and tolerant
- Daring and adventurous
- Open to new things
- Enjoys many varied activities

Worst Traits

- Impractical
- Scatterbrained
- Vain and self-indulgent
- Superficial in friendships
- Dogmatic

ROMANTIC *Profile*

sional pain. Wallowing in self-pity, for tunately, is not your style. Moping is for passive signs! Buoyant Archers rebound quickly, though you'll always remember the dream that got away.

Twenty-something Centaur women prefer the chase to being caught. You tend to see commitment as a trap to be carefully avoided—at least for the time being. (By the way, that's about all you're cautious about.) You may be wildly attracted to the man of the moment, but the thought of permanence casts a certain haze over the thrill of now.

Later in life, romantic idealism may kick in, inspiring you to search for a soulmate—someone to go biking and read Plato or Plutarch with. While largely immune to passing infatuations, Sag falls hard when she falls. The plunge can lead to both heady romance and occa-

Date to die for:
A chance meeting with a tall, athletic-looking French tourist at a New Orleans cafe

To qualify as fantasy material, a man had better be smart enough to hold your attention, sassy enough to talk back to you, and secure enough to give you your freedom. Which

178

doesn't mean you can't be faithful. Sagittarians often settle right down in a relationship...but only if their need for novelty is being sated through alternate means, such as frequent travel or inventive bedroom odysseys. For you, the keys are spontaneity, stimulation, exploration, and—oh, yes—a clearly-marked exit.

Special Rendezvous:
On a misty mountaintop

Your Ascendant Reveals How Others See You

Second in importance to your sun sign, your rising sign determines the image you project. The inner you may be different, but your ascendant guides your automatic reactions to situations.

Aries: bold, impulsive, assertive, independent

Taurus: loyal, stubborn, patient, reliable

Gemini: witty, restless, versatile, talkative

Cancer: moody, cautious, vulnerable, intuitive

Leo: proud, ambitious, passionate, luxury-loving

Virgo: critical, practical, methodical, hardworking

Libra: tactful, refined, intelligent, charming

Scorpio: shrewd, intense, powerful, secretive

Sagittarius: open, restless, cheerful, curious

Capricorn: steady, honest, practical, authoritative

Aquarius: unique, friendly, stubborn, inventive

Pisces: kind, sensitive, adaptable, spiritual

(See Instant Ascendant Locator, p. 252, to locate your rising sign.)

Significant Others

There is no "bad" Sun Sign for lively Centaur girls. But when it comes to building a lasting relationship, some signs suit better than others. Any match can succeed *if both partners are willing to work at it.*

Your Best Bets

As a playmate, **Aries** is peerless—you are the catalyst for his pioneering nature, and the novelty is non-stop. Plus, he has a practical side and doesn't mind paying for those pricey getaways you adore.

Leo, too, is a princely escort who provides plenty of sensual satisfaction. (Just take care not to prick his outsized ego.)

Another **Sagittarius** shares your sophisticated pleasures and is as hot to see the world as you. You could really go places together!

And lively **Libra** is always a lark—until he starts pushing for permanence, that is. You're just not ready to put down roots—at least, not in this garden.

In **Aquarius** you'll find a sweetly inventive lover whose sensual improv never ceases to surprise.

An outside favorite is **Capricorn.** True, he can be tedious—he takes things so seriously!—but his tender, take-charge manner appeals to the part of you that craves protection (mostly from yourself).

Worst Prospects

Taurus is another sensible sort—so far, so good. Trouble is, he wants to cuddle when you want company, then caps your ho-hum evenings together by snoozing in front of his sitcoms. What a yawn!

As for **Cancer,** he's impossibly moody. You may get a kick out of his loony sense of humor, but if truth be told, he can't take a joke.

With uptight **Virgo,** it's talk, talk, talk...he's too shy to take the initiative, and he spooks so easily if you make a move.

Jealous **Scorpio** is dangerous for a genial flirt like you—if you insist on your freedom, you just might get stung.

Pisces, on the other hand, couldn't hurt a fly, but his weepy self-pity leaves you cold...and bored!

Fickle **Gemini** blows hot one week only to freeze you the next. Beware: of all the signs, he's the one most likely to inflict permanent damage, possibly because he initially seems so right.

Passionate
Interests

The Archer's passions are many. For a fiery type who lives to test the limits, the hard part is fitting everything in.

For starters, you're addicted to globetrotting. All destinations beckon, from Aruba to Zanzibar, with special preference given to those that are remote or inaccessible (to others, that is; nothing's too far out for you!). You'll roam anywhere, anytime, alone or with company. You want to see it all...and getting there is half the fun!

Getting in shape is another serious sideline. Whether skiing the marvelous moguls at Aspen or pitching a winning inning of softball, Centaurs feel friskiest while working up a sweat. Competition inspires you, but solo sports are fine, too; you're perfectly able to challenge yourself. The only physical activity

you're not fond of, in fact, is exercise for exercise's sake. AbsRoller and Nordic Track just don't appeal.

When you aren't out discoing or dashing to Dieppe, Archers can be found in intellectual pursuits from studying exotic languages to surfing the Net. Enlightenment is a constant quest! The quest extends to your spiritual side: quite likely you're a member of an organized religion (possibly you've dabbled in several) and an avid reader on subjects from astrology to Zen. Literature per se is less intriguing, though you've a soft spot for mysteries and sci fi. You love to curl up with a mind-bending author while listening to mood-enhancing music (mostly New Age).

And it's not just yourself you're out to improve. Visionary Archers also aim at reforming the planet. Education is your pet project (Sagittarius rules higher learning), but given some zesty issue like the environment or animal rights, you're just as hot to trot. But always in a leading role. Fervent as you are about your worthy causes, you draw the line at mindless busy-work (you know better than to waste your energy and talent). An envelope stuffer Sagittarius is not!

Happiest When...

- walking in a sunny meadow
- teaching a child to whistle
- touring a stable of Arabian horses
- planning a trip to an exotic place
- at a wild west rodeo
- playing competitive mixed doubles with a favorite partner

Wouldn't Be Caught Dead...

- vacationing on a tramp steamer
- playing mah-jong with Aunt Maude
- sleeping all weekend
- following the rules
- whining about a broken nail
- darning anyone's socks

Domestic Style

Though home is seldom where your heart is (more like Hawaii, or maybe Halifax), the Archer's pad is surprisingly inviting. You don't need to *work* on your decor—it's full of fascinating artifacts of your many adventures: souvenirs from exotic trips and eccentric pals. Native American totems jostle for space with a peasant rug from Mexico or the giant papier-mache paperclip by that friend who just made *Art News.* In view of the potential for clutter, you'd do well to hire a cleaning service—fast, before company arrives.

It's never long between get-togethers for you. Archers adore having a crowd over, especially on the spur of the moment (that provides an excuse for the dust bunnies and take-out Thai). Not that you can't cook; you've been known to toss together an inspired pot of paella when so inclined. A masterfully creative chef, you've collected some pretty terrific recipes on your rambles abroad. It's just that you don't often have the time to do them justice.

Anyway, the pièce de resistance at any Sagittarian gathering is the guests. Bank presidents, bunko artists, politicians, priests, pole vaulters—you know them all. And you have a knack for getting them

to mingle, even in the oddest combinations.

That's why you usually feel snuggest in a spacious place. A wide-open loft would suit you perfectly—or maybe a nice little ranch with scads of acreage. If one of those isn't an option, a condo with maid service, convenient tennis courts and pool will have to do. At the very least you'll need a patio garden. Access to the great outdoors is de rigueur for restless, nature-loving Centaur girls. So are possessions that are easily portable (a favorite hammock, laptop, paperback editions of cherished books), just in case you you decide to pick up and move.

After all, given your peripatetic lifestyle, there's never any telling when Hong Kong, or Heidelberg, will call....

The Sagittarius Cook

Tempting, exotic aromas waft from your kitchen. You particularly enjoy experimenting with foreign cuisine: Thai, Moroccan, African...let's give it a whirl! You seldom restrict yourself to a set recipe; you like to toss in a dash of this and a pinch of that, to make a dish your own. Even if you're not a gourmet chef, you're always a great hostess. No one ever goes home hungry from your dinner parties; your portions are generous, and seconds are always offered.

Ten Years From Now...

By now, Heidelberg could be little more than a haunting memory, its most tangible legacy the fluent German you speak! Chances are you've done some sort of extended stint overseas; few Archers don't. And unless you've got a trust fund to tide you over, you probably put in some time teaching English or troubleshooting for a Stateside company to earn your chicken tandoori. The Peace Corps is another popular path for Centaurs; it lets you satisfy the urge to change the world while scratching that travel itch. Your drive to improve things is surpassed only by the need to explore!

Alternately, you might have been exploring the hometown job market, trying some new careers on for size. You may have had as many as four professions in ten years! In any case, one thing you haven't been doing is sitting still. Opportunities seem to increase in direct proportion to the distance from where you started; that fabled luck gets even more fantastic when you're on the move!

Will you be set to settle down after seeing what's out there? That depends.... Footloose Sagittarius never sheds her wanderlust entirely, but you could embark on an odyssey of a different sort. Once you shake the dust off your hiking boots, you might apply those first-rate study skills to Dr. Spock. Centaurs can be the zodiac's warmest, most wonderful parents (though your housekeeping will always be a bit sporadic). Motherhood doesn't dim your bohemian eclat. You still soak up the local culture and go native wherever you are—which is sure to enrich the lives of your offspring.

You don't neglect family duties; they just get added to your infinite interests. You may be juggling babies and a course in Visual Basic, or chairing the latest fundraiser for the Junior League. But you're also the only mom on the block who rollerblades and spends summer vacations on a kibbutz. (P.S. You don't look a day over twenty. Spunky Archers aren't about to let a little thing like time get them down!)

Potential Pitfalls

Here are a few dangerous tendencies you should work to avoid:

- Get-rich-quick schemes
- Romance with a possessive man
- Confrontations with the boss
- Speeding tickets
- Losing a good mate through neglect
- Being smug about a job
- Letting debt get out of hand
- Gabbing when you should listen
- Taking true friends for granted

Your horoscope explores the positions of the stars and planets at the moment you arrived in the world. In your case, the sun was in the tenth house of the zodiac, ruled by the constellation Capricorn. Of all the elements that make up your astrological chart, your sun sign casts the broadest influence, governing your conscious self, so it is the focus of this book.

The eight planets and the moon each exert their own force as well, helping to form your unique and multifaceted personality. (Your moon sign, for example, governs those unconscious desires.) The human body is seventy percent water, and the planets exert a sort of tidal pull, producing certain character tendencies. (That's not to say you can't combat the negative ones if you try, but they are part of your internal make-up.)

The zodiac signs are governed by four elements—earth, fire, air, or water. Your ruling planet is Saturn, the lord of time and discipline who gives structure to the world. In mythology, Saturn was a Titan, son of Gaia, the Earth goddess, so it makes sense that your element is earth. As an earth sign, Capricorn Lady, your feet are firmly planted on the ground. You are dignified, traditional, steady, practical, and hardworking—never given to reckless flights of fancy.

Each sun sign is characterized by one of three qualities—fixed, mutable, or cardinal. Capricorn is a cardinal sign, which means you direct your energy in forceful ways; you are a leader.

Your symbol is the Sea Goat—no ordinary goat, but two animals in one. It has the body of a goat with a tail that is part fish, part serpent. The serpent and fish represent your wisdom and capacity to fathom great emotional depths. (In short, you're very sensitive!) The goat symbolizes your sure-footed ability to climb to the mountaintops of success. Tough and stubborn, Capricorn, you won't rest until you've made it to the top of whatever path you choose—whether that's running the house or running *for* the House.

Your Profile:

Resonant colors: Gray, black, green
Stone: Emerald
Plants: Pansy, ivy
Day: Wednesday
Parts of Anatomy: Bones, skin, joints
Lucky number: 4

Like your symbol, the Goat, you are destined for the top of the mountain. Determined, ambitious, efficient, you will scale the sheerest peaks to achieve success. And if the goal is at the end of a rocky road and a yeoman's years, you don't care. You set your sights on a dream, and nothing gets in your way.

Saturn's child is highly disciplined and wholly realistic; no wonder you succeed! You expect to work hard in order to reach the top. And the top is the lowest you'll settle for. The effort is an essential part of the achievement. After all, that's the right way to do things.

One little problem: all that striving for perfection can make you more than a trifle intolerant. The Capricorn lady tends to be Ms. Critical. Just ask the kid who cuts your grass, or your hairstylist—not to mention a few of your dearest friends, your parents... my dear, the list does go on! (Even you can't always measure up to your high standards!) Try to balance things out by noticing the *good* parts as well.

Saturn's child, your respect for structure and rules give you a strong sense of right and wrong. Most goat girls are very moral (and did we mention a teensy bit judgmental?). There's nothing wrong with firm beliefs, but if you're not careful, you could get so locked into the "right" way of doing things that you become rigid. So try to lighten up!

You're so serious that you sometimes have to remind yourself to use that wicked sense of humor—which can be your lifesaver even if it is usually barbed. It's the best way for you to deal with your anger and your sadness. Saturn's girl can be prone to pessimism and depression, but a good laugh is a great release.

Since your M.O. is work hard, play hard, and always get results, it's no surprise the Goat has difficulty relaxing. When work is your only outlet, you can become isolated.

Then the mood elevator hits the basement. Make a special effort to break up the long work week; it will probably improve your performance. Don't forget to smell the roses as you climb the trellis of success!

Admirable Traits
- Self-Motivated
- Successful
- Pragmatic
- Organized
- Ambitious
- Efficient
- Patient
- Loyal
- Moral

Aggravating Traits
- Harboring resentment
- Self-righteous
- Thin-skinned
- Self-doubting
- Status-driven
- Controlling
- Judgmental
- Critical

Saturn's child is lucky: you can look good in just about anything th catches your eye. And that usua means luxury items—clothes th show the world how successful y are. Try starting with a silk teddy, a layering up with an Armani suit and mink coat. Your planet, Saturn, rul the skin, giving you a penchant f leather: butter-soft suede jacket lizard pumps, and kid gloves a comfort clothes for Capricorns.

Capricorn, you're a classic! No trendsetter, you. Traditional, conservative basics are the ticket—maybe dressed up with a daring bracelet or

You go for colors that are as serio as you are—shades of gray and, course, ever-basic black. Your taste makeup is classic as well: precise, el gant, never brazen or garish—your li flawlessly outlined in red, eyelids ju

> *Saturn's child is lucky: you can look good in just about anything!*

splashy scarf. You'll wait for that trend to pass the test of time before it hangs in your closet, thank you! Your look is timeless, tasteful, with more than a hint of prestige and success.

touched with color, and the comman ing contour of your cheekbon heightened with a single stroke blush. Regal, poised, sensual...tha the Capricorn style.

You're so goal-oriented (in the best sense) that you probably belong to a gym and go exactly three times a week—a good policy for a workaholic! Physical exertion can balance all that brain work you do on the job **and**, by the way, get you out of the office—no easy task. And, of course, good exercise relieves your proclivity toward depression.

We won't catch a goat girl in an aerobics class with twenty other women. You prefer exercise you can do alone, and win at—like running a marathon! Lifting weights is right up your alley; you can chart your progress as you add more weight, and measure your success. Besides, weights strengthen bones and joints, the special province of your ruler, Saturn.

Capricorn's mantra is, *work hard, play hard, exercise hard.* Even letting go has to feel like work for you! Relaxing is something you should do more of, but you don't have to be quite so *intense* about it; it doesn't work that way. Lighten up! Try meditating once in a while. Remember, stress makes you age quicker. So take care of yourself, and you'll be as *ageless* and classic as a great designer suit!

Saturn, your planetary ruler, influences your attitudes, interests, personality, and emotional nature. Here are a few ways Saturn affects you:

- *Ambitious to succeed*
- *Serious about life*
- *Industrious*
- *Organized*
- *Authoritative*
- *Ready to lead*
- *Indomitable spirit*
- *Practical*
- *Loyal in friendship*
- *Intelligent and deep*

With your high standards, high energy, and practical approach, the penthouse office is yours. You're a born businesswoman, Capricorn, destined for a position of authority. Key words: shrewd, efficient, organized, pragmatic, dignified, stable, reliable. You're a rock in a crisis, ever mindful of maintaining a good reputation. Few can compete with your work ethic, good sense, and sheer drive. A smart boss has little choice but to promote—especially since that's what you demand. You relish hard work, but you expect your due. That means promotions, raises, benefits, assistants, maybe a couch for your office! If you're not appreciated, you'll find recognition elsewhere—and you don't hesitate to let employers know it!

That's why you'll most likely wind up in a bigger company where the chain of command is well established. Saturn's child, structure is your security, and you know exactly how to rise through the ranks in controlled, orderly environments. You're the mistress of all trades, but certain areas are particularly good fits. You'd be terrific as an architect, business administrator, rancher (how 'bout goats?), real estate agent, jewelry maker, museum collector, or chiropractor.

Money worries? Not for you, barring some unforeseen catastrophe

(and with your practical, forceful character, even catastrophe is to be efficiently overcome). Since you value money, thrifty lady, you'll always have it. Your financial M.O. is *make plenty, stash some in the nest egg, and spend the rest on the best deals.*

But bargains, for you, are never cheap trendy items. It's always the quality, conservative classics for Lady Capricorn—in attire, autos, or abode. They never go out of style, and they last forever. (You do know where all the half-price outlets are!)

Never a gambler, you lean toward conservative, sure-fire investments—real estate, government stocks and bonds dominate your portfolio. For the perpetual planner, every purchase should have "increasing value" written all over it. For you, even hobbies are an investment; it's part of the pleasure.

Careers to Consider

Your ruling planet, Saturn, tends to draw your sign into certain professions. Typical Goats often excel as:

- *Antique dealer*
- *Politician*
- *Restaurant owner*
- *Dentist*
- *Book binder*
- *Movie producer*
- *Professional organizer*
- *Sculptor*
- *Stage designer*
- *CPA*

With Friends and Family

Like everything else, dear Capricorn, friendship is serious business to you. Which explains why your business rolodex may be bulging but your home phone isn't ringing off the hook. You don't have a flock of fair-weather pals you fly off to Cancun with for Easter. Your friends are few and true blue.

But that's okay; your ruler is the planet of time and time *is* on your side. True friends will stick around long enough to see the real you, and you're worth the wait. You are quietly loyal, in for the long haul, ready with a solution to fix any crisis.

...you have a big heart, but you don't wear it on your sleeve.

Caution dominates the Capricorn girl in matters of trust—even with friends! You're generally too reserved to get down and really exhale. Your dignity comes first, even if it makes you seem a bit aloof. The fact is, you have a big heart, but you don't wear it on your sleeve. It takes time for you to get close to people.

The aquarian half of your Sea Goat symbol gives you amazing intuition that puts you right in tune with the needs of others. You're not just there to share the good times; you'll be available for momentous occasions, good and bad. You're the one who helps pick out your best pal's wedding dress—or helps her through a tough divorce.

It's your nature not to trust until you're sure of someone. Sometimes you need your friends to prove they care. The odd thing is, you rarely ask for a favor; you hate feeling obligated. So ask! Give them a chance to prove it! You know you'd do the same for them. In fact, generous Capricorn, you never say no to a friend. You're happiest when someone needs you. If you can fix a problem, you're in control. And that's when you're most comfortable.

The one thing you hate is a surprise visit, even from your best buddy. Saturn's child, you're guided by structure; anything impromptu goes against your cosmic need to schedule time (right up through your next life)!

One word of caution: high-minded goat girls can get irritated (even vengeful!) over mini-injustices from a friend. No one's perfect (including you!). Don't let your finely-tuned sense of justice puff up into paranoia!

It's not always easy to be your friend. But who cares? You're worth it. Like a fine wine—it takes time and patience to render quality.

Best Traits

- Faithful and fair-minded
- Reliable
- Self-sacrificing, if necessary
- Honorable and conscientious
- Patient and practical

Worst Traits

- Emotionally inhibited
- Secretive and suspicious
- Insensitive to others' emotional needs
- Melancholy; easily depressed
- Controlling

Hello, Capricorn's Crisis Connection.

ROMANTIC *Profile*

want a mate for life. And for the perfect partner you're willing to compromise—sometimes too much. Beware; it's mission impossible for you to give up who you are. Sooner o

Capricorn girl, you're a tough cookie. (Joan Crawford could play you in the movie of your life!) But romance is one dangerous exception. Deep emotions are constantly throbbing to get out. But you don't like feeling vulnerable! Usually, you can cover up the heat with a protective layer of caution—often at a price. Affairs may end before they even start, or wither on the vine when you get too critical!

Once passion takes over, you try in vain to keep control. But control can't protect you from your own heady heat. Romantic figures don't balance out like those in your bank book.

The fact is, dear Goat, you

Date to die for:
Dinner at a tiny French restaurant, squashed into a corner table

later, you'll resent the one you gave it all up for. That doesn't mean you have to choose between a paramour and a profession. You may make some bad investments in the love market. But as always, the Goat sets her sights on the peak and won't dally long on any low road of love.

You need a courtly gentleman caller—someone who'll take the time to learn your nature and win your trust. To cut through your cool, a dream date might come bearing roses and reservations for a quiet little table in the corner. Après date, perhaps some passionate postcards, a couple of meaningful messages in your E-mail...anything to break down your instinctive caution. Once the trust turns on, so does the passion—and if he plays his cards right, it may never turn off!

Special Rendezvous:
Behind your tent
on an archaeological dig

Your Ascendant Reveals How Others See You

Second in importance to your sun sign, your rising sign determines the image you project. The inner you may be different, but your ascendant guides your automatic reactions to situations.

Aries: bold, impulsive, assertive, independent

Taurus: loyal, stubborn, patient, reliable

Gemini: witty, restless, versatile, talkative

Cancer: moody, cautious, vulnerable, intuitive

Leo: proud, ambitious, passionate, luxury-loving

Virgo: critical, practical, methodical, hardworking

Libra: tactful, refined, intelligent, charming

Scorpio: shrewd, intense, powerful, secretive

Sagittarius: open, restless, cheerful, curious

Capricorn: steady, honest, practical, authoritative

Aquarius: unique, friendly, stubborn, inventive

Pisces: kind, sensitive, adaptable, spiritual

(See Instant Ascendant Locator, p. 252, to locate your rising sign.)

Significant Others

There is no "bad" sun sign for steady Goat girls. But when it comes to building a lasting relationship, some signs suit your needs better than others. Any match can succeed *if both partners are willing to work at it.*

Best Prospects

Salt-of-the-Earth **Taurus** could wind up a partner in business *and* the bedroom. You both respect home and security and have deep wells of passion.

High-powered, aristocratic **Leo** might be just the king for Queen Capricorn! He'll court you with Dom Perignon, Godiva truffles, and imported orchids. Heaven!

With **Virgo** you've met someone as realistic and organized (and critical!) as you are, who craves commitment, security, and work—maybe not the most romantic pair but deeply admiring and affectionate.

Look out for **Scorpio**! Your combined chemistry could produce an explosive reaction. You both play it cool until trust is established, then it's obsession!

Another **Capricorn** could be a soul mate—*if* you can both get past your naturally cautious natures. You have a rare romantic rapport, and he totally understands your long work hours.

Free-floating **Pisces** is awfully fun, even though your feet remain firmly on the ground. The Fish accepts your vulnerability, which allows you to trust him. And he can lead you to heights you've never imagined!

Worst Prospects

You won't go far with **Sagittarius.** Commitment looks like a trap to Sag. While you work toward a fixed goal, the Archer flits from job to lover to country (spending money every second!). It's a rare goat girl who wants to keep pace.

Charming, clever **Gemini** is also too unreliable for the steady-as-you-go Goat. Gemini is also too flirty (with *everyone)* and too careless with your feelings.

Cancer is sweet and nurturing, wants a family, and is thrifty as well. But his down moods can be maddening, mostly because you can never get a straight answer about what's bothering him!

Charming and elegant, **Libra** is too hearts-and-flowers for the no-nonsense Saturn girl. Baby talk is a turnoff—if you even get that far. The Scales is so indecisive, he can't decide what to order for dinner.

You might make money with **Aquarius** but you won't make love. He's too busy administering to human-kind to notice one mere person. And he's probably a little too open-minded for the conservative Goat.

At first fiery, sexy **Aries** knocks you for a loop. But alas, the Ram is a big baby who craves the three C's of parenting: cooking, cleaning, and cuddling—not a job for ambitious Capricorn. You just can't take him seriously after a while.

201

For the practical Saturn girl, a proper pastime should never waste time. You see no reason why playtime projects can't accomplish something or produce a yield...like gardening. Your rose garden improves your property value while it makes your home more beautiful. (And you can use the petals to make potpourri for Christmas stocking stuffers!) Likewise, your collection of antiques constantly increases in value every second you admire it.

In literature, too, you expect a return. No fluff for you; you'd rather curl up with a book that will get you ahead. Your bookshelves are bulging with classics, history books, historical biographies. Political satire appeals to your barbed sense of humor (and covers current events).

In music, as in everything, the classics appeal. Television? Maybe the educational channel.

When you do get around to pure leisure (*only* after you've printed out the final draft of that report), it's organized and competitive—cards, bowling, golf. Or you go for high-energy, rewarding activities—hiking and climbing are ideal for goat girls. You'll rarely find Capricorn kicking up her hooves on the dance floor.

You're drawn to craggy landscapes with a sense of challenge: you hear the siren call of those rocky beaches of Maine louder than the whispery soft sands of the Florida Gulf. Your vacations are planned with a purpose. The south of France is not your style. You'll get more out of some historical site—the Smithsonian (again!), the pyramids in Egypt, or the art museums of Rome. You don't often see a Capricorn girl napping under a blanket on a Caribbean cruise. Which is not to say that you don't demand a certain comfort level.

When you do go away, you always make your reservations at an established luxury hotel. You're not going to take any chances on iffy out-of-the way spots, even if they are cheaper. It's worth the extra money to be hassle-free.

Happiest When...
- pruning your hedges
- flea market hopping
- taking an enameling class
- watching presidential debates
- attending a Margaret Meade film festival

Wouldn't Be Caught Dead...
- discoing at the Lizard Lounge
- sunbathing at the nude beach
- watching Star Trek TV Marathon
- gambling in Atlantic City
- in front row at a Boyz 2 Men concert

Domestic Style

Home really is where your heart is. You'd rather buy than rent because you want the permanence and security of sitting in front of your *own* fireplace. If possible, the Goat prefers a quiet street in the suburbs to a bustling neighborhood in the big city.

Naturally, your digs are impressive. You bought your place for its value (resale and status), as well as for practical comfort. After all, a well-made abode won't require as much maintenance. You'd never waste money on shoddy goods...and a rented apartment doesn't announce to the world that you've made it.

Inside, the furnishings are just as solid as your A-frame's structure. When decorating, you look for things that endure, furniture you can put down roots with. You pick

antiques or brand names for lasting value. No Valiant will ever darken your driveway. A Volvo is more like it, for comfort, safety, and prestige.

Saturn girl's decor tends to be cool: leather couches, gleaming (practical) hardwood floors, imported Mexican tiles (durable, easy to clean). Your color scheme is as conservative as

you—shades of beige, respectable grays, elegant greens. No buttery yellow bedroom or even one red wall in the kitchen. A small living room chair covered in rust-colored velvet is about as splashy as Saturn's staid child gets. (You won't find any frou-frou floral throw pillows here!)

So, there aren't many design surprises, but Capricorn's home is always clean, classy, and in good repair. You care about what the neighbors think—and you expect them to care what you think. Whether it's a luxury urban condo or a three-story Victorian in the suburbs, you guard your privacy. Good neighbors do *not* pop by unexpectedly; your life is built on schedules. An impromptu visit makes Saturn's child a fidgety hostess.

When you do entertain it's usually intimate soirees. No food fads for you. There'll be caviar, champagne, and Camembert on the coffee table—never polenta canapés or the latest coffee-flavored beer. There are no awkward surprises on your menus...or on the guest list. That's just the way Capricorn likes it.

The Capricorn Cook

You're a practical cook, always in complete control. You do things right. You can transform an onion, celery, fenugreek, and chicken breasts into a mouthwatering entree—all for about two dollars! Whether the boss or the next-door neighbors, guests always feel welcome at your home. And for a dinner party (small), you'll pull out a recipe that's been handed down through the family—something simple and hearty, meat and potatoes.

205

Ten Years From Now...

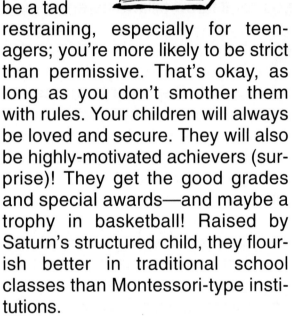

Ten years down the road to the top, all your hard work should be paying off: chances are you're a VP in charge of your department, with a house in the right neighborhood, your children enrolled in the right schools. What did anyone expect? This is just how you planned it—and the best-laid plans of Sea Goats seldom get derailed.

An earth sign, Capricorn women need to put down roots, and yours will be getting deep by now—including a family, your connection between the past and the future. "Family values," like everything else, means something very precise to you. Your children have good manners, always abide by the house rules, and they help take care of the baby or an aging grandparent. You'll make sure they inherit your sense of family and responsibility.

Your super-orderly house might be a tad restraining, especially for teen-agers; you're more likely to be strict than permissive. That's okay, as long as you don't smother them with rules. Your children will always be loved and secure. They will also be highly-motivated achievers (surprise)! They get the good grades and special awards—and maybe a trophy in basketball! Raised by Saturn's structured child, they flourish better in traditional school classes than Montessori-type institutions.

But whatever school they attend, whatever path they choose, they'll probably do well. After all, Mom instilled them with the motto that served her well: Work hard, follow the rules, and get the credit you're due.

Capricorn, you're a lucky gal: you only get better as you go. You look fabulous—in shape and sophisticated. You're more self-confident than ever (if possible!), and wiser. Capricorns take their time coming into their own, and your best years may still be ahead of you. In fact, Saturn's daughters often age in reverse. It's all downhill from here!

Potential Pitfalls

Here are a few dangerous tendencies you should work to avoid:

- Anxiety about the future
- Ignoring your changing needs
- Thinking job success can keep you warm on a cold night
- Neglecting to have fun along the way
- Marrying for your image, rather than for love
- Being miserly
- Thinking practical is always best
- Taking loved ones for granted
- Hyper-conservative clothing
- Trying to control everyone and everything

Fascinating Aquarius, you were born when the sun was in the part of the sky ruled by the Water Bearer. Aquarius represents the future. You're a trendsetter, way ahead of the times with your innovative ways and ideas.

You get along well with all types of people, for you are loyal, stimulating, and very open-minded.

The zodiac is an imaginary belt that divides the sky into 12 sectors. Each is ruled by a different constellation. Your horoscope is a chart showing where all the heavenly bodies were at your birth. To know all about you, we'd need a complete map of the sky, including the moon, Mercury, Venus, and the other planets. All exert a subtle "tidal" pull on us, as they do on the oceans, because the human body is seventy percent water. But the sun is the most powerful force in our solar system. As the dominant factor in the horoscope, it determines the majority of our characteristics. Of course, you get to decide which of those characteristics you want to exploit. The tendencies are there; it's up to you to adapt or reject them to suit your own idea of who you are.

Astrological tradition assigns each sign a gender, quality and element, based on its position in the zodiac. These describe its essential nature. Aquarius is a masculine sign, made of fixed air. The masculine classification denotes your active approach to life (feminine is passive), while the fixed quality means you are strong-willed and resourceful. Your element is air, indicating that your most important activity occurs in your mind.

Uranus, your planetary ruler, is named for the ancient Greek sky god, the lord of the universe. It is the planet of sudden change, nick-named "The Lightning Bolt." Uranus gives you an independent nature, a free spirit, and those little quirks in your personality. (You get a kick out of shocking people.) Uranus's children are full of mischief—and fun!

Your Profile:

Resonant color: Electric blue
Stones: Amethyst, aquamarine
Plants: Orchid, basil
Day: Wednesday
Numbers: 7, 8
Parts of anatomy: Ankles, shins

Your individualism sets you apart from the crowd of ordinary women. They are slaves to fashion; you are always yourself. Undaunted by social norms, you are governed by your own unique thoughts, and sometimes they're pretty wild! Uranus, your planetary ruler, is associated with unpredictable phenomena, such as earthquakes and firecrackers. Your mind is a similar phenomenon. Your planet is also linked to feminism and independence. Aquarian women have emancipated attitudes toward life and love.

Aquarius girls are full of contradictions. You are intellectual by nature and extremely innovative. You come up with all sorts of ideas that are ahead of your time. But in bucking trends, you may develop a stubborn streak and become set in your ways and your thinking. Beware of rebellion for its own sake; it's just another version of conformity.

If you are true to your sign, your habits are somewhat erratic. You tend to take more interest in humanity as a whole than in individual fellow humans. Even small things like returning phone calls seem an unnecessary burden to you! But because you are a humanitarian, genuinely caught up in the fate of the human race, friends who share your concern will forgive your little inconsistencies.

Rules and restrictions are the enemies of rebel Aquarius. You set your own standards and do your best to meet them. You mingle with all levels of society. You have friendships with an amazing variety of people. The best thing is, they all tend to like each other when you're around.

You tend to become bored easily, especially in the company of people less intelligent than you. It's too tedious when your audience can't keep pace with you! Wit is one of your strong points: your sense of humor is bright and sophisticated.

The Aquarian personality is a complex blend of traditional values and progressive ideas. In ancient times, Saturn, the planet of discipline, ruled Aquarius. When Uranus was discovered, it became the sign's modern ruler. Their combined influence produces a curious mix of the conventional and the daring.

It all boils down to this: you respect and keep the traditions you believe in. You toss out the restrictions you consider outmoded. You are the future, unfettered Aquarius woman!

Admirable Traits
- Inventive
- Humanitarian
- Determined
- Sociable
- Tolerant
- Intuitive

Aggravating Traits
- Stubborn
- Detached
- Impersonal
- Rebellious

THE OUTER YOU

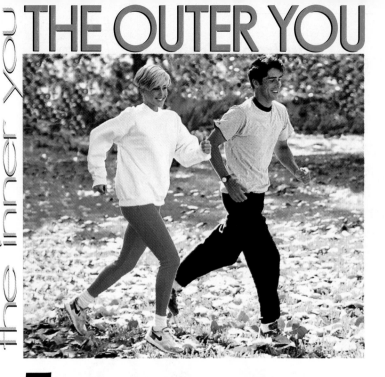

to extremes. It's not healthy to eat on grapefruit or rice for weeks at a tim Your diet should include fish, chees onions, cabbage, and whole gra bread or cereal to provide vitami (B12 and D are essential to acti Aquarians).

Like everything, your health hab are changeable. You often g involved with a project and forget about staying in shape. If anyo else points out your inconsistenc you go on the defensive. Aquarius a fixed sign; you can be stubbor when you want. Still, you could be efit greatly from a quick shape-up ro tine you could do at home or with friend. (Some exercise videos featu

The world's genuine individualists are born under Aquarius. If it's new or different, it appeals to you. So it's not surprising that many food faddists

> *Aquarius is a fixed sign;*
> *you can be stubborn, when you want.*

and vegetarians are found in this sun sign group. Just make sure you don't carry any unconventional eating habits

workouts for couples. That's one w to firm those Aquarius-ruled low legs and ankles, and enjoy doing it.)

There are times when a friend needs your shoulder to cry on in the middle of the night. You'll always be there for them, even at the expense of your rest. But in general, you are sensible and try to get a good night's rest. You don't want to have to face the morning exhausted, so you won't prop your eyelids open just to be polite.

Your independent nature applies to fashion, as to everything else. You're never a slave to passing trends. Sure, you might occasionally buy something just because it's kicky or "in". (What ever happened to the mood ring and the green nail polish?) But you seldom make extravagant purchases of one-time-only clothes. You insist clothes be comfortable as well as attractive. You look terrific in bright colors—even neon orange and poison-green aren't too strong for you. You love to turn heads, and even raise eyebrows, but you seldom err on the side of the grotesque: you have a natural aesthetic sense.

There's no doubt about it: you're one special lady! Uranus influences your thinking, appearance, personality, and emotional tendencies. Here are some examples of its effects:

- *Daring and confident*
- *A rebel at heart*
- *Enjoy "different" people*
- *Need mental stimulation*
- *Independent*
- *Eccentric*
- *Fun to be with*
- *Like gadgets*
- *Enjoy new experiences*
- *Always thinking*

Your innovative flair makes you a valuable commodity on the job market. You're a logical thinker, but you often skip several mental steps and arrive at a creative solution to a problem. Few workers offer employers the rare abilities you provide. Your job should encourage inventive thinking and allow you to put your guiding principles into action.

Professions that serve or benefit the community are ideal for your humanitarian nature. You are a born public servant, with the public's interests sincerely at heart. Or you may enjoy a job in a modern industry such as computers, television, electronics, or space exploration. Aquarians make excellent teachers. Others are fine musicians or comedians. You may even find success as a professional astrologer. If you seek satisfaction from your work, avoid jobs that employ your hands more than your mind.

Bosses and co-workers appreciate your dedication and enjoy your bright ideas and humor. Your unpredictability may be a problem in some professions or with some employers. You need to find a place

where you're not too closely monitored, and where they won't mistake unpredictability for unreliability.

You're not interested in money for power or hoarding. To you, cash is paper you trade for other things that you value more. But your tiny conservative streak, bestowed by Saturn, guides you to set aside some savings for an emergency.

Financially, this is one of the most important periods of your life. You are in a cycle of enormous growth and change. You're just becoming aware of exciting new opportunities to achieve personal goals and to improve the image you project to the world. Jupiter and Uranus bring you chances to resolve some long-standing problems to your satisfaction. Increased self-confidence empowers you to take an important career step you've been mulling over. Now's the time to improve your financial condition.

Careers to Consider

Certain careers are ideally suited to your sun sign. You may enjoy being a:

- *Playwright*
- *Gymnast*
- *Inventor*
- *Photographer*
- *Psychologist*
- *Stunt pilot*
- *Electrical engineer*
- *Aircraft designer*
- *Physicist*

With Friends and Family

Aquarians make truly wonderful friends. But anyone who tries to cling to you, or expects a relationship to be predictable, is in for a huge surprise. You love to meet new people and are instantly at ease with them. People enjoy being with you because you're fun, smart, and accepting. But they soon learn not to expect you to keep all your dates or go out of your way to stay in touch. You can't be burdened with rules about punctuality or returning calls. If pals want to reach you, the onus is on them to keep trying.

probably don't do much socializing with your parents or siblings. Close friends appreciate your non-judgmental attitude about their odd little quirks. (You have quirks of your own and expect their indulgence.) Any pal who

You love to meet new people and are instantly at ease with them... they enjoy being with you.

ing calls. If pals want to reach you, the onus is on them to keep trying.

You most enjoy being with people of your own generation, but older folks often take to you. As an adult you

needs encouragement can be sure of getting it from you. But friends need to be wary of your competitive streak: you hate being overshadowed in your own specialty. And you have zero tolerance for whiners.

You are attracted to individuals who stand out from the crowd. Some of your friends are probably involved with the New Age. They may be interested in yoga, astrology, channeling, tarot or some other such subject.

You're a bit of a loner. Because you feel stifled by too much closeness, you cultivate few intimate friends. You need to relate to others on a deep and caring level, but it takes a while for such bonds to develop. You can enjoy platonic friendships with men.

Most Aquarius gals are drawn to animals, sometimes of an exotic breed. You may have a Sharpei (those wrinkled faces are adorable) or a rare curly Rex cat—something the next-door neighbors have never seen before. But pets aren't just curiosities, to you; you are kind to them.

Co-workers find you fascinating but slightly wacky. Aquarians are bored by bigots. You're likely to speak up if an acquaintance badmouths a race or ethnic group. They may not like being called on it, but they admire your courage and integrity.

Best Traits

- Affable and entertaining
- Lots of stimulating ideas
- Enjoy new places and things
- Bold views and daring deeds

Worst Traits

- Unpredictable about commitments
- Emotionally cool and detached
- Rebellious and eccentric
- Unsympathetic to complainers
- Undemonstrative

ROMANTIC *Profile*

You are definitely unforgettable. You have a brilliant mind that dares to look at love and romance from a different angle. You're the best listener a partner could have, but you also do a lot of the talking. Everyone you meet, without exception, goes under your mental microscope. You never stop probing a new man about everything imaginable.

There's a charming tendency in you to see the good in a partner. Although you're an idealist about love, you also know what's attainable and what's not. But that doesn't keep you from being attracted to people who are out of reach or off limits. It may cause occasional pain, but your motto is, "Nothing ventured, nothing gained." When you love, you accept a partner's

flaws and virtues without illusion or any compulsion to reform. You're not the easiest person to love. Even in romantic relationships, you're independent and detached. This may

> ## Date to die for:
> *Touring the Egyptian section of
> The Chicago Art Museum*

madden or confuse a possessive partner. You need a certain kind of closeness in a lover; he should also be your best friend. What you crave most is a solid relationship based on communication. But you don't want any relationship if it means living with heavy restrictions. You're a people person, who likes new faces. The fascination you hold for other people may threaten an insecure partner.

Marriage is not among the major goals of your life. Many Aquarian girls marry late; some not at all. You go after what you want. If, for some reason, you don't get it, you figure it wouldn't have made you happy. You know better than other signs, there are always new chances to find love.

Special Rendezvous:
On your private plane on a
deserted runway at midnight

Your Ascendant Reveals How Others See You

Second in importance to your sun sign, your rising sign determines the image you project. The inner you may be different, but your ascendant guides your automatic reactions to situations.

Aries: bold, impulsive, assertive, independent

Taurus: loyal, stubborn, patient, reliable

Gemini: witty, restless, versatile, talkative

Cancer: moody, cautious, vulnerable, intuitive

Leo: proud, ambitious, passionate, luxury-loving

Virgo: critical, practical, methodical, hardworking

Libra: tactful, refined, intelligent, charming

Scorpio: shrewd, intense, powerful, secretive

Sagittarius: open, restless, cheerful, curious

Capricorn: steady, honest, practical, authoritative

Aquarius: unique, friendly, stubborn, inventive

Pisces: kind, sensitive, adaptable, spiritual

(See Instant Ascendant Locator, p. 252, to locate your rising sign.)

Significant Others

There is no "bad" sun sign for idealistic Water Bearers. But when it comes to building a lasting relationship, some signs suit your needs better than others. Any match can succeed if both partners are willing to work at it.

Your Best Bets

 A love match with another **Aquarius** features mental stimulation and devotion. It's always changing, never confining. You both know that intimacy isn't the opposite of freedom. You'll love being together.

 **Gemini** has never met a woman so easy to get along with. You've never met a man so eccentric. You amuse and stimulate each other. Good match.

 **Leo** woos you in style; his showy gifts are a kick! He shouldn't try to understand you. He should just experience you. Through love and patience, this partnership can succeed.

Aries is awed by your humanitarian impulses; you're overwhelmed by his list of achievements. A pretty good partnership all around.

Libra has never had so much undivided attention. You make him feel clever and important by really listening to his ideas! This relationship has great potential.

Sagittarius is as independent as you are. He's riveted by your many interests; you enjoy his enthusiasm. A fun-loving and compatible combination.

Worst Prospects

Taurus eats different things, does different things, and wants different things. Any common ground is purely accidental. One of you would have to sacrifice too much.

Cancer craves closeness; you need space in a relationship. He enjoys quiet evenings; you are comfortable in groups. He'll make you claustrophobic.

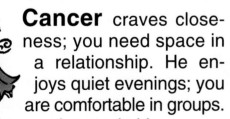

Virgo is embarrassed by your unconventional style; he has a way of making you feel as odd as a third arm. Best to keep this on a "just friends" level.

Capricorn is a practical man; you're a dreamer. You are fascinated by people; he's mainly concerned about himself.

Scorpio's intensity is wasted on you. After a while it's just too much of a good thing. While he's making love to you, you may wish you weren't missing your favorite television show.

Pisces dwells on the past; you focus on the future. You're friendly and objective; he's aloof and sentimental. You'll always be pulling in opposite directions.

Passionate Interests

Unusual activities appeal to you—and anything you've never done before is likely to win out over something you have. You could enjoy anything from skydiving to collecting Victorian bell-pulls.

Whatever your hobby, you get deeply involved in it. Star-gazing fascinates many Aquarius girls. You may have a fancy telescope on your deck. Chances are you're an amateur astrologer.

When you have the money and time, you travel for mental stimulation and a needed break from routine. Guided tours are not your style; you don't want to worry about keeping to a set schedule. You'd rather feel free to spend an extra day at any place you find especially interesting.

Aquarian girls are more intellectual than athletic. Sports appeal to you chiefly as a spectator. You enjoy watching a good basketball or baseball contest, even if you've never held a bat in your life. But something out-of-the-way would be even better. Soccer or rugby or polo is more of an adventure—and a good place to spy some handsome hunks.

Your concern for humankind is a guiding force, and you probably support many charities. You gravitate toward less popular causes. If you have a favorite, it's likely to be a support group or an animal welfare society. And you won't just throw money at a problem. Many Aquarians march to increase awareness of a charity or to raise funds for favorite causes.

Your reading list features anything out of the mainstream—gossip newspapers, science fiction, and horror stories probably appeal. If there's a hint of the supernatural, so much the better! New Age publications dealing with chakras, crystals, or astrology intrigue you. Your taste in art, as in everything, is highly individual. You appreciate the beauty and grace of exquisitely done bronze statues of animals or cowboys. Aquarian musical preferences tend to be equally eclectic. You enjoy romantic instrumentals, electronic music played on synthesizers, chant, or exotic instruments.

You dream of going off on a great adventure. Pursue it. Cruising the Nile in an old-fashioned paddlewheel boat would be a blast! Be sure to take a big hat, shades, sunscreen and a camera to record your holiday. King Tut awaits!

Happiest When...
- at a spontaneous party
- turning heads with an outrageous dress
- visiting an exotic place
- living by your own rules
- changing someone's mind

Wouldn't Be Caught Dead...
- in a shouting match
- joining a racist group
- ordering sushi
- standing on line at Planet Hollywood
- pining for the past

Domestic Style

Your home reflects your unusual interests and delightfully different personality. You like spacious rooms with lots of windows for a bright, airy atmosphere. The furnishings you choose reveal cultured tastes and advanced ideas. For the walls, you prefer fresh colors: white, buff, pale yellow, light blue, or other pastels. An uncluttered look suits you, but tidiness is not your strongest trait.

Home, to you, is a central base from which to go out. Household chores bore you. You spend more time intending to clean than you do actually getting down to business. On the other hand, many Aquarian girls are better at small home repairs than the average male Aquarian.

You tend to be particular about certain cherished items. (That pyramid you bought during your New Age phase and the strange shell you picked up on your vacation are still somewhere in your possession.) Your partner or roommate learns quickly not to touch these treasures.

Wherever you live, you look for mental stimulation. When you entertain friends, you serve the latest new snack and lots of sparkling conversation. Theme parties are a good ice-breaker; you might host a "Come as Your Favorite Comedienne" party. But you prefer being a guest at parties. Hosting involves too much work, preparation, and stress—and there's not enough time to mingle and chat. You're a better guest than hostess. Luckily, you get lots of invitations; everybody loves having you at their parties.

Much as you love society, you need lots of time to yourself. When you want to be alone, you find a quiet place and tune out the world—sometimes for days on end.

Strange things occasionally happen at your address, but you don't let them worry you. Weird events make great conversation pieces.

And if your lifestyle differs from the norm, so what? You'd rather be off the wall than boring, any day!

The Aquarius Cook

You experiment in the kitchen and enjoy trying exotic recipes. Ever an innovator, you produce sometimes a masterpiece, sometimes a disaster. When things go wrong, you have material for a new tale to tell. It's such fun to sample different foods. (Tofu? Been there, cooked that! Cajun? Did that ten years ago.) You enjoy sampling ethnic foods and odd combinations, and if you don't have one ingredient, you'll daringly substitute something else. Eating at your home is always an adventure.

Ten Years From Now...

There's no predicting the unconventional, adventurous Aquarius girl. If she can't find a career that's far-out enough, she'll probably invent one. You may have been working with the world's foremost maker of roller coasters, having a barrel of laughs and some hair-raising rides. (Maybe you personally designed the ZigZag Fireball, a combination sea-and-sky ride, now the leading attraction at the latest film studio/amusement park.) Or you could have decided to set up spiritual retreats in Kalamazoo, Kansas City, or even Kyoto, where visitors can go to find inner peace.

A two-year stint with the Peace Corps would be no surprise for Uranus's child. Learning new customs and language provides the novelty you crave—and just think of all the stories you have to tell your friends! Chances are any decade will involve at least two careers and a dozen adventures for any Aquarian.

Now you're getting ready to launch a new career…or maybe you'll settle down and start a family. Several hot prospects are out to win your love...but will you be content to settle down with one partner, after seeing what's out there in the wide, wonderful world? Think carefully. Freewheeling Aquarius never loses her need for change entirely, but raising a family is an adventure in its own right, and kids are an endless source of variety!

On the other hand, there's that standing invitation to design a music therapy program at the local rehab center. One thing is certain: you won't lack for ideas! Maybe you'll move to Alaska and start a family there, where you can experience the aurora borealis. Or you might settle down in the Southwest, where there's still room to stretch your wings. Most Aquarians have an affinity for spectacular scenery and open spaces. And who knows? You might run into a soul mate!

Whatever happens, you'll always be the blithe spirit of the zodiac. You commit to a relationship—or anything else—only when it suits you. And you're wise, Aquarius. You know what you want to do. What's more, you'll do it!

P o t e n t i a l   P i t f a l l s

Here are a few dangerous tendencies you should work to avoid:

- Becoming too rigid in your thinking
- Giving up on getting close to people
- Thinking new always means better
- Trying too hard to be different
- Dodging responsibilities
- Ignoring a parent's good advice
- Marrying someone different just for shock effect
- Letting your mind go to waste
- Expecting special treatment to suit your quirks
- Failing to get in touch with emotions

pisces

The zodiac divides the sky into twelve zones, each ruled by a different constellation. At the time you were born, the sun was in the twelfth position in this imaginary belt, which makes your sun sign Pisces.

Your horoscope is determined by many other factors as well: the placement of the other eight planets and the moon puts its imprint on your personality. However, your sun sign is the most influential of the planetary forces that make up your astrological chart, for it affects your conscious self.

As the last sign of the zodiac, Pisces is a fascinating jumble of qualities from all the other eleven signs. This mix endows you with great versatility and rare intuition.

Each sign belongs to one of

four elements—air, fire, water, or earth. Pisces, naturally, is a water sign; your ruling planet is Neptune, the Roman god of the oceans. In astrology, water represents emotions. Pisces's emotional depths are as boundless as the sea.

Your intuitive powers are like radar; you pick up tiny signals all around you and respond deeply to everyone and every situation.

The symbol of Pisces is two fish tied together, swimming in opposite directions. Your sun sign signifies your dual personality. Your life is a balancing act (and sometimes a struggle) between the practical world of reality and the rich world of your imagination. Often pulled between desires, Neptune's child is unpredictable in behavior—one minute a placid lake, the next a tempest-blown sea.

The heavenly bodies also endow

each sign with a quality, which determines how you use your energy. Pisces is a mutable sign (as opposed to fixed or cardinal). That means you use your energy to transform. There's a duality to this quality, too: you can be easily influenced, *but* you can also change the world (for the better!). That's you: Pisces, a delightful, complex combination of complementary qualities.

Your Profile:

Resonant Colors: Aquamarine, reddish purple
Stones: Chrysolite, ruby
Plants: water lily, seaweed, moss
Lucky number: 11
Part of Anatomy: Feet
Day: Sunday

Who are you, anyway, Pisces girl? You're as difficult to describe as your element, water: fluid, elusive, constantly changing form.

One thing's for sure: everything is possible with you. A dreamer, you live in the Land of Imagination—and others love it when you carry them with you on your magic carpet of fantasy!

Everyone loves being with you because you become the person you're with. You can speak commercial-ese with an investor who might back your play, or chat intimately with an avant-garde sculptor about the effect and meaning of his style.

But wishy-washy? You? *Au con-traire*! It's just that everything is so relative. Each choice has its good points, and you see them all too clearly. So how to decide on just one? Easy. You don't.

'No boundaries' pretty much describes you all over: you're just a girl who can't say no. Every out-of-work actor with a hard luck story has your number. (Take in one more stray cat and you'll be evicted!) Don't forget to take care of yourself, devoted Pisces. All that altruism can drain you like a vampire, and your main recovery system is to withdraw. Better set aside regular intervals of space and time for just you—which means saying no, if only on occasion.

Daughter of Neptune, whatever you're doing, your moods can shift like the tide. One moment, you're riding a crest of confidence, then suddenly—for no reason—you may feel totally inadequate, or dragged under by some vague sense of guilt.

As your spirits plunge, a haze of romantic dreams rolls in to break the fall. Be careful not to get lost in the fog and end up ignoring everything you meant to do. Usually dreams alone are enough to produce this state of happy oblivion, but beware of other tempting ways to drown your troubles. Go easy on the cocktails, and whatever you do, don't reach out to the first romantic distraction that comes along!

Hopeless procrastinator? May as well 'fess up! Sidetracked by a fascinating story on the A.M. news, you might forget to finish dressing. Before you know it you're late for work. Don't try *too* hard to curb that wandering mind; its next journey may lead to inspiration. But remember: a few daily routines and contact with friends can keep you balanced enough to rise above the blues.

Admirable Traits
- Accepting
- Responsive
- Generous
- Perceptive
- Imaginative

Aggravating Traits
- Inconsistent
- Moody
- Unrealistic
- Lacking self-confidence
- Procrastinating

THE OUTER YOU

As for the right clothes to enhanc your charms, you look great in an thing! Your mutability lets you loc right in a motorcycle jacket—or mink coat. Some people put on a outfit; you can put on a whole ne personality. Your favorites, thoug are loose-fitting clothes. Fish ha anything restricting their free-floatir movement. Severe cuts are too co fining for you. Flowing five-pleate pants are more your style...or thos filmy balloon pants you saw at th "Song of India" boutique. They let yc show off your shape-changing natur

Neptune's children are renowned for riveting beauty, and it's not just on the surface! Men get lost in your soulful eyes, entranced by the uncommon

Pisces rules the feet, and Neptur women like to treat them right. Call yc

> *Some people put on an outfit; you can put on a whole new personality.*

ideas they see there. There's an aura about you—mysterious, magical, magnetic—that makes you instantly irresistible!

the Imelda Marcos of the zodiac: shoe are your obsession! You have dozer of pairs for every occasion! Spare pai are stashed everywhere, just in cas you need a change of style.

In clothes or cosmetics, your palette is shimmery: oceany greens and blues, anything at the end of the color spectrum (mauve, purple, violet). And always pastel; Pisces is so sensitive to color that pale is plenty.

Fitness for its own sake is not your thing. Even if you gained 10 pounds last month, you won't be running to join the gym (or running anywhere, for that matter)! You're just not the athletic type… except for swimming (like a fish). Health problems, for you, usually start in your head: negative thoughts, the product of an over-worked imagination. Then the balance between your mind, body, and spirit gets knocked out of whack. Exercise can help release the tension.

Speaking of mental health… you may have a tendency to eat (or even drink!) with your emotions. Food can be a comfort in times of stress, but a huge plate of pasta and a bottle of Chianti may be too much of a good thing. On the flip side, never go on a deprivation diet. It's a sure way to upset that mind-body balance, and Pisces needs to keep an even keel.

Not that the Fish is ever beached for long. A naturally strong constitution and a knack for metamorphosis can always get you back in the swim!

Neptune, your sign's planetary ruler, influences your appearance, personality, emotional nature, and approach to life. Here are some examples of its effects on you:

- *Imaginative lover*
- *Sympathetic toward friends*
- *Gentle with animals*
- *Softly curved face or body*
- *Sensitive to criticism*
- *Enjoy quiet places*
- *Fond of the sea*
- *Secretly shy*
- *Strongly intuitive*
- *Remember rejections*

Adaptable and creative, Pisces woman, you can handle anything in the career sphere… except a set routine. Predictability is a stagnant pond to the Fish. Best career picks employ your creativity, imagination, or sensitivity (preferably all of the above).

The creative currents carry lots of Pisces women into the entertainment biz and the arts (including the healing arts, like medicine and counseling). But you don't need to be the star. The fish often prefers a supporting role—make-up artist for a photographer or set designer for a theater company. You're more likely to write screenplays or advertising copy than your own memoirs.

Whatever you're doing, you probably need to work up some courage and ask for raises due you. "What's the salary?" is not the first on your list of job interview questions. You're more interested in how you're going to stay interested for eight hours a day. To Neptune's child, money isn't important; only what you do with it. And what you do is spend it. (If you even *have* a savings account, nothing stays in it for long.)

Like everything else, your spending is ruled by your emotions. If you *love* that cashmere sweater, you'll take one in every color, please.

You'd sooner pop off to Portugal on a whim (even at prime rates) than plan six months ahead for a cheaper package tour. Timing is everything, and you don't want to risk losing the impulse.

Luckily, my dear, you *dread* poverty—otherwise, you might end up there. However much you have is how much you tend to spend. When the coins get low, you get thrifty (well, thrift*ier)*. Major debt isn't your line—but neither are nest eggs.

Not that you have a lot of trouble making money. It's just that the cash flow fluctuates. The freelancing Fish can make a packet on a project, provided she's fascinated. If your interest wanes, your bank account will, too. But you're wise enough to scout out a new gig when supplies are running low.

A couple of money drains you could plug: "Lending" a loser a few bucks (generosity is among your best points, but you could be more selective), and letting your lover decide your investments. Romance and finance don't make the best mix. Consider getting a broker instead to make some wise investments. Then you and your man can fantasize about how to spend the dividends!

Careers to Consider

Certain careers are ideally suited to your sun sign. You may enjoy being a:

- ***Romance writer***
- ***Museum curator***
- ***Bartender***
- ***Probation officer***
- ***Guidance counselor***
- ***Interior decorator***
- ***Librarian***
- ***Hospice worker***

With Friends and Family

Fabulous Fish, you may not always make great *romantic* choices, but friends are a different story. You are a true and loyal friend, and you attract the same kind. Bosom buddies open up to you, and they are rewarded. How many times have you heard, "You're the only one I can trust!"? You alone know the deepest darkest details of many a soul. You were the first to know about your girlfriend's affair with her boss; your cousin confided in you alone when he was going bankrupt.

nature gives you a passkey to other people's feelings. Everyone leaves your tea and sympathy sessions feeling enlightened as well as unburdened. After one or two of your direct-hit insights, *voilà!* Everything is crystal clear.

You are a true friend.... You alone know the deepest darkest details of many a soul.

Neptune's daughter can carry a sea of secrets! Understanding, sympathetic, you make everyone feel totally accepted, no matter what terrible truth they're dying to spill. Your mutable

Being such a perfect friend can overextend you. Carrying so many burdens, even if they're not your own, can be draining, and you may get anxious and need to withdraw. You want time to recoup? No big deal. No one minds your "I want to be alone" mode. They just wish you'd warn them *before* you stop answering the doorbell.

Regenerating is one thing. Turning reclusive is another. Alone for too long, your vivid imagination can run amok to some pretty dark places. Never mind that you *chose* to shut your door; you get to thinking your dearest friends don't appreciate you after all. If they did, they'd surely be pestering you to find out what was wrong. And what about that new coworker...why does she keep discovering all your little mistakes? Is she after your job? Beware: when you're in a "mood" (with a capital "M") you put everyone else in one, too, and they may feed your paranoia.

Don't worry so much! You just need a little balance. Get a good night's sleep. Dream about ways to pace yourself (and learn to say no)! And remember, friendship is a two-way street. Your friends could help you (the way you help them) but not if you iso-

late. You can't expect them to read your mind, even if you can read theirs. You need to do a little outpouring yourself. Talking or listening, Pisces, you are the original soul mate!

Best Traits

- Kind and devoted
- Adaptable; varied interests
- Emotionally responsive
- Sensitive to others' needs
- Patient

Worst Traits

- Hypersensitive
- Negative attitude
- Impractical
- Insecure
- Moody

ROMANTIC *Profile*

Pisces, you love being in love. Doesn't matter who or what or how long. You just want to be moved. And there's no predicting your type. Chances are it's someone completely different each time. Intensity and variety mark the Pisces lover's style. You immerse yourself in each relationship like an actress in a role—costume and all! Date a baseball fan, and soon you'll know all the scores—and be wearing a baseball cap! No slow courtship or cautiously dipping your toes; you look deep into his soulful eyes and action—a sizzling romance with all the trimmings.

Your fantasies demand champagne, music, roses in bloom, and a runaway passion worthy of the setting. But all that atmosphere isn't always the formula for a happy ending. Your craving for drama often pairs you with unsuitable costars. When the lights of reality come up, they may be all too harsh in contrast with your dream world. When that happens, you're off to the next picture show.

Date to die for:
Skinny-dipping in chilly water on a moonlit night... you'll find ways to keep each other warm

---

You're beautiful, passionate, and fascinating, but you're not easy (nothing worthwhile is)! As in other things, you tend to swoop from highs to lows, and your lover may not enjoy the ride. If he can't provide the emotional reassurance you need, you'll have to seek elsewhere. You must have someone who will let you pour out all your feelings. (Just make sure you're really expressing what they are.)

Somewhere in your mind's golden eye, you can see your perfect soulmate, and you truly expect to meet him. But when you do, he'd better know how to approach. A net is the wrong style for this Fish; suspecting a trap, you quickly dart away. A shiny lure (with no hook) is better bait for Pisces. Once you do find Mr. Right, don't worry about getting bored. Your deep craving for variety and change simply won't *let* the romance go stale.

Your Ascendant Reveals How Others See You

Second in importance to your sun sign, your rising sign determines the image you project. The inner you may be different, but your ascendant guides your automatic reactions to situations.

Aries: bold, impulsive, assertive, independent

Taurus: loyal, stubborn, patient, reliable

Gemini: witty, restless, versatile, talkative

Cancer: moody, cautious, vulnerable, intuitive

Leo: proud, ambitious, passionate, luxury-loving

Virgo: critical, practical, methodical, hardworking

Libra: tactful, refined, intelligent, charming

Scorpio: shrewd, intense, powerful, secretive

Sagittarius: open, restless, cheerful, curious

Capricorn: steady, honest, practical, authoritative

Aquarius: unique, friendly, stubborn, inventive

Pisces: kind, sensitive, adaptable, spiritual

(See Instant Ascendant Locator, p. 252, to locate your rising sign.)

Significant Others

There is no "bad" sun sign for idealistic Fish girls. But when it comes to building a lasting relationship, some signs suit your needs better than others. Any match can succeed *if both partners are willing to work at it.*

Your Best Bets

As a soul-mate for **Pisces,** who else but another Fish? You have everything in common, but beware of that paranoid streak: you can't help each other if you hit a low together!

Cancer uniquely understands your emotions. But the Crab can get awfully claw-y. If you can get him outside his shell—and get him to let you swim free—it could be good.

Sagittarius is a kindred spirit. His optimism gives you confidence, and he can laugh away your tears and fears. One downer: Sag's bluntness can hurt.

Leo is your dream mate: a romantic, protective hero who finds you captivatingly sexy! You can transform the world into a magic place. Just be sure you give him the royal homage he believes he deserves.

The minute you meet **Scorpio,** it is a magnificent obsession. He's so intense—and you can match him! He's secretive, too, but that's okay; you don't tell all, either. But if he tries to throw a net over his Fish, you'll turn tail and swim away fast.

Romantic **Libra** also sees the world through champagne-colored crystal. He might like things too close for your comfort, but when your nerves wear thin, he'll always offer a sympathetic shoulder.

Worst Prospects

There's action and variety with **Gemini.** But he speaks from his head, you talk with your heart. And he doesn't take your moods seriously. Up to you to decide whether he's worth it.

Virgo recognizes your creativity, but he's so cool and orderly, so un-poetic. He could support you while you paint your masterpiece, but eventually he might resent your sleeping in.

You and **Aquarius** share a need for freedom, and you both want to make the world a better place. But he's too detached; you can't seem to touch him. If he donates all his time to the suffering masses, he may not have any to spare for you when you feel needy.

The fire and energy of **Aries** are dazzling; he takes the lead like a hero on a white charger. But he can be selfish and brash, and bursts in on your feelings without knocking. He might work as a friend, but these injuries are hard to forgive in a lover.

Taurus loves to take care of others. But the Bull needs control (a no-no for you). And you can't pry him away from the TV. He's sweet, but he'll bore you to pieces in no time.

Speaking of boring, workaholic **Capricorn** may give you financial security, but the realist Goat doesn't fathom the Fish's watery world of dreams and fantasies.

241

What does the Fish love to do? Anything to do with water! Water skiing, boating, fishing, swimming, scuba diving—or just lying on the beach and listening to the waves splash the shore.

When you're not taking an ocean cruise to Tangiers, you're out improving the world. You recycle, serve Thanksgiving dinner at a homeless shelter, organize a reading group at your church (if you have a religion, it's probably something unorthodox).

For your own soul you do photography…and, of course, watercolors. You might be seen weekends on the stage of an amateur theater group. Or dancing anywhere, anytime—in a disco club or ballet class. Even alone at home! You love to put on a Coltrane CD and dance an interpretation of his lament!

Your musical taste is as changeable as your personality—from Peruvian pipe music to Paganini to punk. And when you're not playing Mozart on the box, you're likely to be playing your piano (a remnant of a past fling with a classical musician.)

Pets appeal to the compassionate Pisces gal. You always seem to have one (or more)—usually the runt of the litter, or a scrawny stray you saw trying to tip over a garbage can. Or an odd one that tickled your fancy (perhaps an iguana). And, of course, you love fish!

Positively passionate about the movies, you'll only watch them on the big screen. Preferred genres are fantasy films and old gothic romances. (*Wuthering Heights* is your all-time favorite flick.)

You like to curl up in bed with a book: some philosophy, a psychic or astrological study, or the latest translation of the Mayan hieroglyphs. On another night, though, you may be in the mood for a heavy romance novel or travelogue.

Speaking of travel, it's a true passion—but spontaneity is a must. Just charge the ticket, and you're off. But the Fantasy Queen's most passionate interest? Daydreaming . . . what else?

Happiest When...
- photographing nature
- working for a cause
- helping a needy stranger
- receiving a confidence
- starting a romance

Wouldn't Be Caught Dead...
- in a man-tailored suit
- vacationing in the desert
- signing a ten-year contract
- following the rules
- scene-stealing
- putting all your earnings in an IRA

Domestic Style

Pisces' place is warm and welcoming, a comfortable and comforting place to come. Big or small, pad or palace, it's tasteful and not terribly tidy. You're more interested in *living* in the house than cleaning it.

Your furnishings are original and highly artistic. The colors coordinate. (If you have an orange chair, it works!) Silk pillows complement a tweedy couch (lots of textures in the Fish's abode).

Neptune's child likes her environment to be as soft as water: scarves draped over the lampshades to soften the glare of the light bulb, some small Oaxacan rugs to cover the hard edges of the end tables, filmy drapes to filter the sunlight. Whether very modern or very old, your furniture is always comfortable. The operative mood in Pisces' house is relaxing.

Most of the *objets d'art* around the house were not acquired as investments. They simply mean something to you. There's that Christmas ornament your nephew made for you when he was three. And the chipped champagne glasses—you got them for your twenty-first birthday (the best birthday of

your life)! And that portrait of you was painted by your best friend during her first year in art school.

Their placement doesn't follow any rigid decorating formula. Something could hang on the wall one day, lean on the mantel the next, and be sitting on the floor a week later. Depends on how you feel—or how the house feels to you. (Flexibility is a must: no straight-backed chairs around a formal dining room suite at your house.)

Scheduled entertaining is sporadic, but friends are always coming and going. Everyone is welcome. Unless, of course, you're isolating. Then you just pull the shades, put on the answering machine, and ignore the doorbell—until you feel sociable again. Your emotional response to food determines what you fix for dinner. A dinner party menu could change at the last moment because it no longer appeals to your taste. In fact, any-

thing at the house of Pisces could change at any moment. And that's half the fun of going there.

The Pisces Cook

The "depends on how you feel" attitude covers food, too. The fridge may be full, yet nothing in it tempts you. For highly imaginative Pisces, eating is like being in love. It should be an intense, interesting experience every time—rich with spice and variety, and loaded with good associations. (You love birthday cake because everyone is so happy eating it.) You're an imaginative cook, working intuitively, sensing which seasonings blend well. No wonder guests so often request your secret recipes!

245

Ten Years From Now...

By now, you may have visited all but one of the seven continents (by boat, of course). You have probably been in and out of at least five amorous relationships; a Pisces girl never outgrows her need for variety, and that could take the form of quantity over quality. But if one face stood out in the crowd, you will have settled down with someone who provides all the spice your life needs. One thing's for sure, Pisces: you'll never accept boredom.

In any case, you've got a family, whether it's spouse and kids or just large groups of friends. Close kin and bosom buddies, you tend to spoil them all. (Your mouth still hasn't mastered shaping the word *no.)*

If you have kids, they're lucky! They'll share the variety of experiences you pack into your own life. You'll haul them to this museum and that concert. They'll have music and dance lessons, study yoga—maybe spend a summer excavating a tomb in Egypt. That's the fun stuff.

Your toughest parenting task will be discipline. It's just not in your mutable nature to be firm or consistent. Be careful, dear Pisces: you can confuse the poor kids with your vacillations. Not that any guilt is required! There's no such thing as a perfect parent, and you have many more gifts than shortcomings. Especially when they reach their teens, your children will appreciate your empathy and intuition when they find it hard to express—in words—all the conflicting emotions they are feeling.

Like your symbol, you're still trying to swim off in all directions. You want it all, both ways, everything at once. Do take care that you don't get swamped trying to be a perfect wife, homemaker, mother, and career woman. When the details of life number one too many and stress strikes, just say "no" (or at least, "wait a minute"). Then head for a steamy bubble bath and replenish your energy in your watery element. That'll keep you feeling as young as you look.

Potential Pitfalls

Here are a few dangerous tendencies you should work to avoid:

- Bank overdrafts
- Seeking comfort in food and drink
- Controlling lovers
- Becoming obsessed with hurts
- Taking health for granted

- Self-doubt
- Boring clothes
- Scattering your energy
- Falling for flattering con men

Aries Celebrities

Maya Angelou
Paula Abdul
Emma Thompson
Andrew Lloyd
Webber
Gloria Swanson
Paloma Picasso
Leonard Nimoy
William Shatner
Pete Rose
Olivia Hussey
Dennis Quaid
Betty Ford
Kitty Kelley
Linda Hunt
Christopher Walken

Taurus Celebrities

Candice Bergen
Sigmund Freud
Cher
Salvador Dali
Tori Spelling
Michelle Pfeiffer
William Shakespeare
Barbra Streisand
Natasha Richardson
William Randolph
Hearst
Janet Jackson
Audrey Hepburn
Bianca Jagger
Shirley Maclaine
Fred Astaire

Gemini Celebrities

Joan Collins
Siobhan McKenna
Isadora Duncan
Carroll Baker
John F. Kennedy
Clint Eastwood
Marilyn Monroe
Andrea Jaeger
Billie Whitelaw
Joyce Carol Oates
Barry Manilow
Isabella Rossellini
Gena Rowlands
Martin Landau
Wallis Simpson

Cancer Celebrities

Karen Black
Estée Lauder
Oriana Fallaci
Diana Rigg
Norma Kamali
Lena Horne
Eva Marie Saint
Jerri Hall
Abby Van Buren &
Ann Landers
Shelly Duvall
Barbara Cartland
Kim Darby
Ringo Starr
Anjelica Huston
Giorgio Armani

Leo Celebrities

Vivian Vance
Jacqueline Onassis
Sally Struthers
Delta Burke
Jerry Van Dyke
Emily Bronte
Lucille Ball
Neil Armstrong
Lana Cantrell
Connie Stevens
Whitney Houston
Danielle Steele
Linda Ellerbee
Christian Slater
Elaine Boosler

Virgo Celebrities

Mother Teresa
Claudia Schiffer
Marlee Matlin
Rebecca DeMornay
Kitty Wells
Gloria Estefan
Lily Tomlin
Valerie Perrine
Pauline Collins
Jane Curtin
Swoosie Kurtz
Agatha Christie
Maurice Jarre
Anne Bancroft
Sophia Loren

Libra Celebrities

Linda McCartney
Julie Andrews
Donna Karan
Michael Douglas
Madeline Kahn
Carrie Fisher
Rex Reed
Elke Sommer
Patti Labelle
James Herriot
Sigourney Weaver
Christopher Reeve
Suzanne Somers
Margaret Thatcher
Johnny Mathis

Scorpio Celebrities

Meg Ryan
Bo Derek
Jane Alexander
Annie Potts
k.d. lang
Goldie Hawn
Ruby Dee
Jodie Foster
Cleo Laine
Jeremy Brett
Whoopi Goldberg
Grace Kelly
Nadia Comaneci
Sally Field
Julia Roberts

Sagittarius Celebrities

Woody Allen
Jane Austen
Kim Basinger
Ludwig van Beethoven
William F. Buckley, Jr.
Walt Disney
Chris Evert
Jane Fonda
Florence Griffith-Joyner
John F. Kennedy, Jr.
Margaret Mead
Bette Midler
Brad Pitt
Charles Schulz
Steven Spielberg
Tina Turner
Henri de Toulouse-Lautrec

Capricorn Celebrities

Paula Abdul
Kirstie Alley
Marlene Dietrich
Faye Dunaway
Ava Gardner
Diane Keaton
Susan Lucci
Pamela Sue Martin
Dolly Parton
Victoria Principal
Diane Sawyer
Donna Summer
Howard Hughes
Martin Luther King, Jr.
Humphrey Bogart

Aquarius Celebrities

Helen Gurley Brown
Jane Seymour
Muriel Spark
Eartha Kitt
Janet Suzman
Mia Farrow
Princess Caroline of Monaco
Alan Alda
Cybill Shepherd
Tom Selleck
Farrah Fawcett
Greta Scacchi
Virginia Woolf
Charlotte Rampling
Ronald Reagan

Pisces Celebrities

Cindy Crawford
Judy Garland
Liza Minnelli
Deborah Raffin
George Washington
Sharon Stone
Elizabeth Taylor
Ivana Trump
Vanessa Williams
Albert Einstein
George Harrison
Edna St. Vincent Millay
Diana Ross
Edward Albee
Elizabeth Barrett Browning

Instant Ascendant Locator

The sign on the eastern horizon at the moment of your birth is your ascendant.

Mathematical calculations would be needed to find your exact ascendant, but here's a 90% accurate do-it-yourself method. (If you were born during daylight saving time, subtract one hour from your birth time.)

1. Trace the outer circle (the one showing the times) on paper. Cut out the center.
2. Place the cut-out circle over the inner circle (showing the sun signs).
3. Line up your sun sign with your birth time.
4. The sign at the 6 a.m. position is probably your ascendant.

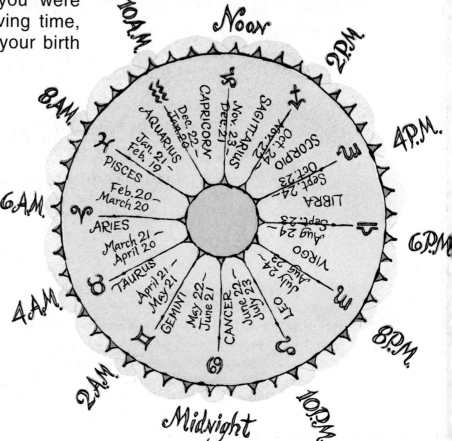